ATTACK
AMERICA ON

Ray Comfort

Bridge-Logos *Publishers*
Gainesville, Florida 32614 USA

Dedication

To my good friends
Denny Ermel, Todd Friel, and
my brother Phillip.

Unless otherwise indicated, the Scripture quotations in this publication are from the King James version of the Bible.

Nostradamus: Attack on America

by Ray Comfort
Copyright © 2001

Library of Congress Catalog Number: pending
International Standard Book Number: 0-88270-882-1

Printed in USA by:
Bridge-Logos *Publishers*
Gainesville, FL 32614
www.bridgelogos.com

Contents

Introduction

On September 29, 2001 the History Channel deemed the prophecies of Nostradamus to have enough credibility to give them the Saturday night prime time slot. The 1981 Warner Brothers documentary stated that Nostradamus warned of fanatical Muslims that would attack New York and blow up its skyscrapers.

Did Nostradamus actually predict the attack on the World Trade Center on September 11, 2001?

Did he actually say,

> *In the year of the new century and*
> *nine months . . .*
> *In the city of York there will be a*
> *great collapse,*
> *Two twin brothers torn apart by*
> *chaos?*

What about his other propecies?

Did Nostradamus prophesy the assassination of President Kennedy?

Did he say that man would land on the moon, and that someone named Hitler would lead Germany?

Did he mention America by name?

Did he have anything to say about the beginning and outcome of the Third World War?

Come on a journey into the acclaimed prophecies of the world's most famous prophet and find out the source of his predictions.

1

Grave Consequences

On a dark night in France during the height of the French revolution, three drunken soldiers took turns at digging a grave. They were about to exhume the remains of the prophet Nostradamus; buried two centuries before. Legend said that whoever drank from his skull would inherit his magical powers. Another familiar legend warned that the same person would instantly die.

Fear had kept the grave undisturbed from those who had been tempted to try the cranium beverage until that dark night in May 1791.

After the intoxicated men lifted the half-rotted coffin out of the grave, they raised the lid to see a sight that paralyzed them with fear. Across the skeletal remains, held in the bony fingers of the prophet lay a plaque that read "May 1791." Nostradamus, predicted the very date of his exhumation.

Undaunted by the plaque, one of the drunken men filled the skull with wine and lifted it to his quivering lips. Suddenly he dropped to the ground. A stray bullet from a riot during the revolution struck the man through the head and killed him instantly.

Unpretentious Beginnings.

Michel de Nostredame, better known by his Latin name, "Nostradamus," was never at a loss for words when it came to that which was yet to come.

The parents of Nostradamus celebrated the birth of their son on December 14, 1503 in Saint Remi, in southern France. His family was Jewish, though they lived in a Roman Catholic country. The Roman church had persecuted thousands of Jews from 1420-1498, calling them "the murderers of Jesus Christ." Shortly after Nostradamus' birth, Louis VII ordered all Jews to be baptized as Catholics or "suffer the consequences," so the Nostradamus family decided to be baptized, but they secretly held on to their Jewish beliefs.

In his early childhood, young Michel went to live with his grandfather, Jean, where he learned the classics and how to speak Latin, Greek, and Hebrew. It was while living with his grandfather that he developed skills in mathematics and as an astrologer. Both his grandfathers worked as personal physicians to the French king, and encouraged his interest in astrology.

As years passed, young Michel studied philosophy, grammar, and rhetoric under the eyes of Roman Catholic priests. He also cultivated his interest in ways of divining the future:

> In his free time he could be found
> in Avignon's renowned papal library
> sampling a wide selection of occul-
> tic and astrological books.[1]

When Michel's father objected to his son's astrological activities, the grandfather suggested that the young man should become more involved in herbal medicine. He was therefore sent to study at the University of Montpelier in 1522, where he amazed fellow students and teachers with his lectures on astrology. He was also said to have expounded at this time his teaching on the earth being round and on its revolving around the sun, roughly seventy years before Galileo (1564-1642) supported the same theory. He graduated with his baccalaureate degree in 1525.

Nostradamus did not appear to be a man of great importance. "He was a little under medium height, of robust body, nimble and vigorous," wrote Jean Aymes de Chavigny, a biographer of the prophet.

> He had a large forehead, a straight and even nose, gray eyes which were generally pleasant but which blazed when angry and a visage both severe and smiling. . . . By nature he was a taciturn, thinking much and saying little, though speaking well in the proper time and place: for the rest, vigilant, prompt, and impetuous, prone to anger, patient in labor.[2]

When the bubonic plague broke out in France, he tirelessly moved throughout the country among the sick, prescribing herbal cures, fresh air, and fresh water. It was here that he gained a reputation as a "healer of afflicted ones," and was sent for by towns from all over Europe. It was his courage and his unusual, yet successful treatments that led to his initial recognition and following.

As his reputation grew as a doctor, so did his fame as a psychic. The nobles and the wealthy of his day began to frequent his home for their horoscopes.

In the mid-1530s, Nostradamus married and his wife bore him two children. Then in 1537, the plague visited his home and tragically took his entire family. This was the blow of a two-edged sword upon his life. The plague not only tore his loved ones from his hands, but damaged his reputation as a physician. Despite his previous accomplishments people could not respect a man who was inable to heal his own family.

An Idol Joke

Shortly before the death of his family, Nostradamus had made a casual but life-changing joke to a workman who was casting a bronze statue of the Virgin Mary. He alluded to it in reference to the "casting of demons." This was later reported to church authorities, who called him to stand trial on a charge of blasphemy. After losing his family and having no desire to face the Roman Catholic Inquisitors for his small indiscretion, he fled east to Italy, avoiding the church for the next six years. It was during this time that his prophetic powers began to manifest them-selves.

Ten years later, he returned to Salon in France, where he settled for the rest of his life. Soon after, he married a rich widow named Anne Posart Gemelle. By day he lived as a "good Catholic," but by night he burned the candles as he consulted his ephemeris and delved into the mystics. He would empty his mind of all thought and gaze into a water bowl where he saw visions of the future.

After some time, he published an almanac which became so successful, he marketed one each year for the rest of his life.

As his fame spread, he told a friend that he would publish a book of the prophecies of mankind, which would tell of future events until the end of time. The publication would be called *The Centuries*, made up of ten volumes, each containing one hundred quatrains (four-line poems) and total one thousand predictions for the future.

He began his work on *The Centuries* on Good Friday in 1554, and soon after published the first volume. Work on the entire publication was completed in 1558. Although he was praised by royalty, other books began appearing which condemned him as a con man. His house was even stoned regularly by zealous Roman Catholics.

As time passed, his writings became widely known. One prediction greatly increased his fame. In *Century* 1, quatrain 35 (C1, Q35) he had warned:

> *The young lion will overcome the older one*
> *On the field of combat in single battle*
> *He will pierce his eyes through a golden cage*
> *Two wounds made one, then he dies a cruel death.*

This was acknowledged as a prediction of the death of King Henry II of France, which is said to have taken place two years after the prophecy was given. In the summer of 1559, the King was jousting with Montgomery, the captain of the Scottish guard. On the third encounter, the lance hit the King's armor, shattered, and a splinter entered the King's golden visor, going into his eye and then into his brain. Another splinter is said to have gone into his throat "two wounds made one." He died an agonizing death ten days later.

A Royal Welcome

A story is also told of Catherine de Medici, Henry II's wife, visiting Nostradamus at midnight sometime before the king's death. It is said that in the flickering candlelight, he motioned her into a magic circle drawn on the stone floor. In front of the circle stood a mirror, upon which were inscribed four names of God written in pigeon's blood. Nostradamus then took the Queen's hand and began singing an incantation to an angel in order to stir up the spiritual realm.

Suddenly, the image of the Queen's first son began to appear in the mirror and as quickly as it came it disappeared, signifying his coming death. Then an apparition of her second son appeared. It circled the room fourteen times, then disappeared, signifying that he would reign fourteen years before his death.

Finally, an apparition of her favorite son appeared and circled fifteen times, then disappeared. The Queen was horrified that her beloved son would be taken after only fifteen years. Afterwards she asked the prophet if the mirror might have deceived them, but he insisted that it could not lie.

During the meeting, an apparition was manifested and seen by the Queen and Nostradamus, which spoke of the king's death. Henry's accident supposedly came to pass a short time afterward.

Francis II thus succeed his father Henry on the French throne, and died after about a year as king. Catherine's second son, Charles IX, thus became king in 1560 at the age of ten and ruled until 1574 fourteen years. Catherine and Henry's third son, Henry III, then became king in 1574. He was stabbed on August 1, 1589 by a fanatical friar and died the next day, having reigned as king for fifteen years.

However, it was the fulfillment of his words in the death of King Henry II that gave Nostradamus fame throughout all of Europe. In 1560, he became the court physician under Charles IX and continued as an advisor to Catherine de Medici, plotting her and her families horoscopes, probably up until his death in 1566.

2

Supernatural Sources

Knowledge of the future strongly hints of some sort of divine influence. It means that perhaps we are not alone on this ball-shaped lump of dirt spinning through space. It means that if we can see that this man's prophecies were accurate in the past, we can rely on them to tell us what is about to take place in the future. That is a comforting feeling.

Jean-Charles de Fontbrune, the author of a number of books on Nostradamus, explained the relationship between prophecies and the common people in this way:

Prophecy then becomes a source of comfort, a refuge for all those ordinary folk who have been sucked unwillingly into the whirlpool of conflicts over which they have virtually no control or at least a strong defense case for the existence of God, the Supreme Being. Through-out history, one of man's most enduring characteristics has been to acknowledge the existence of some force greater than himself.[3]

Did Nostradamus Hear from God?

As with most people who have the gift of seeing into the future, Nostradamus seemed convinced that its source was divine. He said of his inspiration:

Although for a long time I have been making predictions of events which have come to pass, naming the particular locality, I wish to acknowledge that all have been accomplished through divine power and inspiration.[4]

His religious belief was that mankind, represented by Adam and Eve, fell from union with God into a state of forgetfulness. The way back was by studying the Tree of Life, a mystic path with ten levels of consciousness, similar to some eastern religions.

In March of 1949, Henry C. Roberts, the author of *The Complete Prophecies* of Nostradamus, spoke of the prophet's methods by saying:

> Beyond a shadow of doubt, the methods employed and results obtained by Nostradamus in looking to the future were outside of the physical framework.

> What to the contemporary critics of this day, for want of a better term they chose to call magic or occult, we today now recognize as the operation of certain tenuous and imponderable laws that permeate the entire Cosmos. These intangible but all pervading forces we group today under the general title of *Extra Sensory Perception.*[5]

Author of the book *Nostradamus: Countdown to Apocalypse,* Jean-Charles de Fontbrune, goes even further and says:

> Nostradamus states once again: "a small flame comes out of the solitude and brings things to pass which should not be thought vain." Here he is alluding to the Holy Spirit, symbolized by the tongues of flame descending to the Apostles' heads at Pentecost.[6]

In a letter addressed to his son,
Nostradamus again affirms that his prophecies
came directly from God the Creator:

> Sometimes God the Creator by the
> ministers of His messengers of fire
> and flame, shows to our external
> senses, and chiefly to our eyes, the
> causes of future predictions, signify-
> ing the future event, that will
> manifest to him that prophesies. For
> the prophecy that is made by the
> internal light, comes to judge of the
> thing partly with and by the means
> of external light. . . . The reason is
> evident why that he foretelleth
> comes by divine inspiration, or by
> the means of an angelic spirit,
> inspired into the prophetic person,
> anointing him with vaticinations
> [predictions or prophecies].[7]

However, Nostradamus' methods bring the
divine origin of his visions into question. In
Century One, Quatrain One (C1 Q1),
Nostradamus gives details as to how he
received his prophecies:

> *I sit at night alone in secret study*
> *Resting upon the brass tripod:*
> *A thin flame comes forth from the*
> *solitude*
> *Making successful that which*
> *should not be believed in vain.*

C1 Q2 reveals even more:

> **The divining wand in hand is**
> **placed in the middle of the tripod's**
> **brass legs**
> **With water he anoints the hem of**
> **his robe and foot:**
> **Fear! A voice is heard. He trembles**
> **in his robes:**
> **Divine splendor. The divine one sits**
> **nearby.**

Nostradamus would sit on a brass tripod with his spine erect, using the fact that he was uncomfortable in that position, to remain alert. The tripod's legs were placed at the same degree angles as the pyramids of Egypt this was supposed to create a bioelectric force that sharpened psychic powers. Another tripod was placed at his feet, filled to the brim with steaming water and stimulating oils. Then he would do incantations, after which he would do other things essential to the practice. He then tells what happened:

> I emptied my soul, brain and heart of all care and attained a state of tranquility and stillness of mind which are prerequisites to predicting by means of the brass tripod . . . the prophetic heat approaches . . . like rays of the sun casting influences on bodies both elementary and non-elementary . . . human understanding,

being intellectually created, cannot
see hidden things unless aided by a
voice coming from limbo by help of
the thin flame ... from which comes
a clouded vision of great events, sad
and prodigious and calamitous
adventures approaching in due
time.[8]

It is believed that this technique helped
Nostradamus overcome a strong barrier of
fear, which came upon him before he surrendered his will in the "trance of seeing," of
which he says:

Although the everlasting God alone
knows the eternity of light proceed-
ing from Himself, I say frankly to all
to whom He wishes to reveal His
immense magnitude infinite and
unknowable as it is after long and
meditative inspiration, that it is a
hidden thing divinely manifested to
the prophet by two means: ... One
comes by infusion which clarified
the supernatural light in him which
predicts by the stars, making possible divine revelation; the other
comes by means of participation
with the divine eternity; by which
means the prophet can judge what
is given to him from his own divine
spirit through God the Creator and
His natural intuition.[9]

In a preface to *Nostradamus: Countdown to Apocalypse* by Jean-Charles Fontbrune, Elizabeth Green has this remark about such trances:

> Instead of that annoying word "trance" we have a modern term, *abaissement du niveau mental,* coined in the early days of psychology to describe the lowering of the threshold of consciousness that occurs naturally in sleep and fantasy, and unnaturally in delirium, drugged states, and psychosis. For Nostradamus this meant opening himself to visions from God about the future. For the modern explorer of the human psyche it means opening oneself to the archetypal images in the depths of the unconscious. Of those depths we know perilously little, save that, in the light of research by such giants as Jung,[10] the unconscious can indeed be prophetic, not only in the personal terms but in universal ones as well.[11]

Though Nostradamus here and in other places gives credit to the God of the Bible for his insights, his practices look like nothing done by prophets recognized by Christianity, Judaism, and Islam such as Moses or Isaiah. In fact, his method of obtaining prophecies is better reflected in the ritual practices of Branchus, an occultic Greek prophetess. According to Francis X. King,

> throughout these two quatrains [C1 Q1 and C1 Q2] Nostradamus was describing a variant of a divinatory magical rite . . . described by Iamblichus of Chalcis, who died about a.d. 335: "The prophetess of Branchus either sits upon a pillar, or holds in her hand a rod bestowed by some deity, or moistens her feet or hem of her garment with water . . . and by these means . . . she prophesies." This passage, which describes a divinatory rite involving the wetting of a foot and the hem of a garment, was clearly being referred to by Nostradamus.[12]

Darker Sources

The word *occult* means "beyond the realm of human comprehension . . . mysterious . . . secret . . . hidden . . . concealed."[13] Though such things fall into the realm of the supernatural (the "beyond the norm of things in nature," if you will), occultic practices have always had more to do with ghosts, goblins, and demons than the God of Creation. Just what was Nostradamus into? There has always been a mystery surrounding this incredible man, both in his life, and in his death. Just how did he obtain his strange prophecies? Were there forbidden and bizarre practices he performed in the secrecy of his study? Is that why he concealed many of his writings by burning his books later in his life?

Author Francis X. King said this of his practices:

> There is evidence to be found in the curious forty-second quatrain of *Century One* that makes it seem quite certain that Nostradamus had some knowledge of both the darker aspects of the occult arts and of modes of divination involving the use of basins.... That technique was described by the Neoplatonic philosopher Psellus as follows: "There is a type of predictive power in the use of the basin, known and practiced by the Assyrians.... Those about to prophesy take a basin of water, which attracts the spirits of the depths. The basin seems to breathe as with sounds. . . . The water in the basin . . . excels . . . because of a power imparted to it by incantations which have rendered it capable of being imbued with the energies of spirits of prophecy . . . a thin voice begins to utter predictions. A spirit of this sort journeys

where it wills, and always speaks
with a low voice."[14]

If this voice is related to the God of the
Bible, then we should be able to find examples
in this ancient text of similar things happening
to prophets there. Examination of Biblical
texts do indeed reflect similar examples, but
they seem to suggest something rather different about the nature of a spirit that "always
speaks with a low voice:"

> And they shall say unto them that
> have familiar spirits . . . that peep
> and mutter. . . .

> And thy speech shall be low out of
> the dust, and thy voice shall be of
> one that hath a familiar spirit.[15]

Again, the shared opinion of many
scholars about such "familiar spirits" would
suggest that what Nostradamus was involved
in had little to do with the God of Creation.
Look at this dictionary definition of a
"familiar spirit" such as the above texts suggest
Nostradamus was in contact with:

> [A] *familiar spirit* is a divining demon
> present in the physical body of the
> conjurer. . . . The term "familiar" is
> used to describe the foreboding
> demon because it was regarded by
> the English translators as a secret
> *(famulus)*, belonging to the family
> *(familiaris)*, who was on intimate

terms with and might be readily sum-
moned by the one possessing it.[16]

As we look at the stories associated with
this French prophet, they seem to imply contact with the darker side of the spiritual realm.
Remember the story of Queen Catherine de
Medici as told in the previous chapter? A
magic circle, cold stone, mirrors with the
names of God written on it in pigeon's blood,
and the calling forth of an "angel"? Look how
similar it is to this story where instead of a
Queen, a King sought counsel through a
psychic.

King Saul contacted a spirit through a
medium, after vainly seeking God in prayer for
guidance about an upcoming battle. He said
to his servants, "Seek me a woman that hath a
familiar spirit, that I may go to her, and
enquire of her." After his servants found a
woman, he disguised himself and went to her.
When he came, she warned him that such
practices were condemned by Jewish law,[17] but
he promised her protection. He then asked her
to summon the spirit of the prophet Samuel
who had died some time before. When a
hooded spirit appeared standing before her,
she suddenly knew the identity of the king,
and she was again afraid. Saul ignored her and
sought counsel from the spirit, but all that was
told him were predictions of his coming
doom.[18] Saul and his son, Jonathan, did

indeed die in the upcoming battle leaving his family without an heir to the throne.

Such evidence strongly suggests that Nostradamus was doing more than just dabbling in the occult, and that it may have been the source for much of his prophetic inspiration. However, despite this, he continued to assert his innocence at the criticism that his visions were not God-given. On June 27, 1558, Nostradamus wrote a comprehensive letter to King Henry II. In the epistle he answers his contemporary critics:

> Only the Eternal God, who is searcher of men's hearts, being pious, just, and merciful, is the true Judge of it: Him I beseech to defend me from the calumny [accusations] of wicked men. . . . Notwithstanding those in whom the malignancy of the wicked spirit shall not be suppressed by length of time, I hope that after my decease my work shall be in more esteem than when I was alive.[19]

But if his inspirations were indeed more occult than divine, or even somewhere in between, why deny it? Because occultic and psychic practices weren't understood and accepted in his day the way they are today. As the authorities of the time were still burning people at the stake for sorcery, it was most necessary that he convince the king that God Almighty was the sole origin of his revelations. His letter continued:

> I confess truly, that all comes from God, for which I give Him thanks, honor, and praise, without having mixed anything of that divination . . which proceeds not from fate but from God and nature.[20]

Another Alternative

There is of course the possibility that Nostradamus' prophecies came from occultic sources, but Nostradamus mistook them for the voice of the God of the Bible. After all, the beliefs and practices of the church, the only accepted source of spirituality at the time, varied widely as their main unifying text, the Bible, was forbidden for anyone except priests to read. Could Nostradamus simply have been seeking insight from God through any means he could find in the texts that were available to him? Could it have been that he was simply mistaken about the true nature of his   practices? Remember that it was while studying with a Catholic priest that he first began studying books on astrology and occultic   practices. Could he have just seen the occult as another means of communicating with the Power of the universe, as many seem to say it is today?

The question of the source of inspiration for Nostradamus' prophecies is an important one, but not one we can answer before we look further into the nature and substance his predictions. However, I think as we look at more of the writings of this amazing man that we will find the prophet's true source is something far more powerful in its ability to predict the future then what we have already discussed. In fact, Nostradamus actually hid this source for reasons we will explore later.

3

Famous Prophecies of a Famous Prophet

If it is possible, Nostradamus' "hope" that he would be held in higher esteem after his death than during his lifetime, has become truer than his prophecies. If you look on the Internet you can find sites dedicated to his work, and most libraries have at least a handful of the dozens of books that have been written about him in just the last twenty-five years. He was the subject of a major Hollywood motion picture. Tabloids quote him. Video stores carry documentaries on his work. His life and prophecies have even appeared with the famous on A&E's Biography. This may be why:

> With the passing of time, we have come to realize that Nostradamus accurately forecasts a host of happenings, ranging from an English naval blitz on Spanish treasure ships at Cadiz to Adolf Hitler's machinations of war; from the invention of the submarine, airplane, and Montgolfier balloon to the era of space stations and nuclear war.[21]

Add to these predictions the invention of the radio, the light bulb, the great fire of London, the Kennedy assassination, man landing on the moon, the recent attack on New York, and even the naming of America in prophecy. It's no wonder he is so highly acclaimed.

It is amazing to think that a man who died in 1566 may have seen things that people who died in 1966 did not. If they are true, they must take on a new weight of importance. Elizabeth Greene begins the preface to a book about the prophet, comparing his words to those of holy writings: "The prophecies of Nostradamus are as indestructible as the Revelation of St. John."[22] Perhaps what Nostradamus said is more acceptable in such a comparison. If we accept that what St. John saw in his "revelations" on the island of Patmos around 100 a.d. are also for this or a near future time, then it is not so far-fetched that Nostradamus could see such things as well around 1550.

The gift of prophecy is both fascinating and comforting at times. Look at the esteem given to Nostradamus by Jean-Charles Fontbrune:

> We must not despair. If we had only the analyses of the politicians, doomswatchers, demographers, sociologists, and economists to go by, man's horizon would be completely blocked. Absolute and irreversible pessimism would be the rule. The only remaining hope is the prophetic message brought to man. Whether the prophets are those of the Old or the New Testaments, Christ or Nostradamus, they all announce the realization of the "Kingdom" when universal peace shall at last reign among men.[23]

Now look at how incredibly some of the things Nostradamus wrote in his *Centuries* match up with things that we have seen happen since Nostradamus' death.

Some Twentieth Century Predictions

Here is the outbreak of the AIDS virus:

The dreadful war which is
prepared in the west,
The following year the pestilence
will come,
So horrible that neither young nor
old
[shall escape]. (C9 Q55)

This quatrain is a computer virus:

A thing existing without any senses
Will cause its own death to happen
through artifice.
(C1 Q22)

The submarine-launched Trident missile during the Gulf War was even seen by the prophet:

When the traveling earthly and
watery fish
Is thrown upon the shore by a
great wave
Its strange from wild and
horrifying
From the sea its enemies soon
reach the walls.
(C1 Q29)

In 1998 the first parts of the International Space Station were sent into orbit. The station is expected to be fully operationally by 2005. Here is what could be Nostradamus' description of it:

> ***Samarobin one hundred leagues***
> ***from the hemisphere***
> ***They will live without law, exempt***
> ***from politics.***
> *(C6 Q34)*

Here is Reagan, and Gorbachev (complete with the birthmark on his head-last line):

> ***One day the two great leaders will***
> ***be friends,***
> ***Their great power will be seen to***
> ***grow:***
> ***The New Land will be at the height***
> ***of its power,***
> ***To the man of blood the number is***
> ***reported.***
> *(C2 Q89)*

The Swastika

Most of us associate the swastika with the Nazis. However, it was long in use before Hitler picked it up. It has been used in Hinduism and was also used in Germany before the First World War as a symbol of the mythological god Thor. Hitler reversed the position of the arms in the 1920's and employed it as the badge of his corrupt movement. Nostradamus saw this swastika:

> *The great Priest of the Party of*
> *Mars*
> *Who will subjugate the Danube*
> *The cross harried by the crook . . .*
> *(C6 Q49)*

The Invention of the Radio and the Light Bulb

> *When the animal is tamed by man*
> *After great efforts and difficulty*
> *begins to speak,*
> *The lightning so harmful to the*
> *rod*
> *Will be taken from the earth and*
> *suspended in the air*
> *(C3 Q44)*

Many have interpreted the animal in this quatrain which is tamed by man "after great efforts and difficulty" begins to speak, to be the radio.[24] The lightning is the light bulb.

Experts tell us the prophet saw visions of the light bulb and other inventions with such clear illumination, he was more than likely tempted to bring them into his own time. He must have struggled as he tried to put into words the inventions of the future, three hundred years before they'd come to pass.

More Amazing Stories

It is said that in 1534, after Nostradamus fled from the wrath of the Catholic church to Italy, his prophetic powers became apparent. A story is told of him falling on his knees before a young Franciscan monk named Felix Peretti and addressing him as "Your Holiness." This prompted mockery from those who witnessed the event. They were aware that this man was not holy at all. He was just a former pig farmer from a humble background.

However, in time this lowly monk became Cardinal of Montalto and in 1585-nineteen years after the death of Nostradamus-was proclaimed Pope Sixtis the Fifth.

Another story is told that while the budding prophet was lodging at the castle of the Lord of Florinville, the skeptic decided he would test his prophetic powers. While they were strolling one day, the nobleman asked Nostradamus to predict the fate of two barn-yard pigs, one white and one black. Nostradamus replied that the man would eat the black one and that the white pig would be devoured by a wolf. Secretly, the man had his cook kill the white pig and serve it for supper.

After the meal, the nobleman revealed what he had done, but the prophet so insisted that he was correct, that they called for the cook. It was then that they found out what had happened. The cook had obeyed his master and killed and prepared the white pig. But as it sat ready for the oven, a wolf snuck into the kitchen and began eating the pig. Fearing the wrath of his master, the cook killed and prepared the black pig and served it. Thus Nostradamus' prediction was validated, and his reputation grew.

Yet another story is told of Nostradamus suffering an attack of gout. He was confined for ten days and wanted to be alone. Suddenly, there began a persistent knocking at his door. It was a page of the illustrious family of Beauveau, who had lost a fine dog that had been entrusted to him.

Before the page could say why he was even knocking on the door, Nostradamus called out, "What's the matter, king's page? You are making a lot of noise over a lost dog. Go and look on the road to Orleans. You will find it there, led on a leash." When the page turned, he found a servant leading the dog back.

To call such predictions and stories incredible or unbelievable is not far-fetched, but such is the legacy that Nostradamus left for himself.

More Unbelievable Predictions

Here is what is commonly accepted as his vision of World War II:

The machines of flying fire
Will come to trouble the great
commander of the besieged:
Inside there will be such sedition
That the overthrown will be in
despair.
(C6 Q34)

Here are the periscopes of Nazi submarines:

Where he thought to breed famine
there will come plenty,
While the eye of the sea watches
like a greedy dog;
For one to the other will give oil,
wheat.
(C4 Q15)

Here are the fighter pilots:

They will think they have seen the
sun at night,
When they see the pig half-man:
Noise, song, battle, fighting in the
sky perceived:
And brute beasts will be heard to
speak.
(C1 Q64)

The seer also saw submarines:

When the fleet can swim under water.
(C3 Q13)

He even foretold a time when people would travel safely by land, air, and sea:

Pestilence extinguished, the world becomes small
For a long time the lands will be inhabited in peace.
People will travel safely by air, land, seas, and wave.
Then wars will start again.
(C1 Q63)

Once again Nostradamus gives amazing insights into things that didn't exist until hundreds of years after his death. But, it is worth noting at this point that Leonardo da Vinci (1452-1519) foresaw and even sketched the helicopter. He predicted the machine gun and the parachute—which he called the "tent of linen." He formulated Isaac Newton's laws of motion well over a century before Newton (1642-1727) was born.

The Franciscan monk Roger Bacon (1220-1293) even foresaw what could be interpreted as ocean liners, cars, planes, and deep-sea divers. In 1875, Jules Verne foretold when buildings would be a thousand feet high, and spoke of air and underwater travel. In 1899, H.G. Wells predicted automatic doors and a time when religion would be marketed "like soap powder."

These also are amazing predictions, but none of these men claimed divine contact to receive them nor do we regard them as prophets in the traditional sense. As we noted in chapter one, Nostradamus espoused that the earth was round and not flat while he was at university in the 1520s, but there are few among us today that do not remember that "In 1492, Columbus sailed the ocean blue" to prove the same thing.

Can we possibly read these quatrains and their interpretations and not be somewhat skeptical? After all, at closer examination, many of them do seem kind of vague and could be interpreted a number of different ways. Will these supernatural prophecies hold up under the scrutiny of a closer look?

4

Incredible Stories

There are many tales of "supernatural" happenings that cannot be scientifically substantiated. Take for example the three shepherd children near the Portuguese village of Fatima during the First World War. On May 13, 1917, three little girls (seven, nine, and ten years old) told a story of seeing a "beautiful lady from heaven" who talked to them for several minutes.

The vision promised to return, and we are told it did so five more times, on the thirteenth of each of the following months. It wasn't long before 50,000 miracle seekers flocked to the "sacred" spot. Who was this lady? It was reported to be none other than the Virgin Mary. As the crowd stood spellbound, the Virgin gave three messages of forthcoming events. But of the 50,000 who went there to witness the miracle, the only ones who saw Mary and heard her voice were the three girls.

The beautiful lady gave the children a message, which was to be written down and sealed, and not to be opened until the 1950s.

> It was later reported that Pope Pius XII had opened the message of Fatima: but no statement from the Vatican was forthcoming . . . unofficial sources rumored that the Pope had fainted when he read the contents of the letter.[25]

What are we to make of such stories that are based more on rumor than verifiable facts? Such things make fascinating reading and great documentary material, but how often do we find out that the actual circumstances bear little resemblance to the stories?

The Test of Truth

In the early twentieth century, many were profiting from a rebirth of interest in spiritualism and the occult. Rumors ran wild and many were attracted to seances and fortune tellers by the amazing things that were happening at such meetings.

Harry Houdini, the great escape artist, decided to put their claims to the test and see if there was truly any way to contact people who had passed over to the other side. For several years he sought a real connection to the spiritual world, but in all that time, all he did was expose the tricks of this trade, showing the proclaimed mediums to be frauds. He was often able to recreate their "spiritualistic" phenomena and explain them in nonmystical, physical terms. Before he died he even arranged a definitive test of spiritualism. He devised a ten-word code that he would communicate to his wife, if possible, within ten years after his death. After he died, various people maintained that they were able to establish contact with him, but none was able to transmit to his wife the prearranged code.[26]

What are we to learn from this? Simply that we should know better than to believe everything that we hear or read. Historical facts stand up to scrutiny. We may not be able to verify them word for word, but we can get a reasonable idea through documents and other historical recordings whether or not they happened. As with the spiritualists in Houdini's time, fantastic stories became more fantastic with the retelling.

We may see this in the age of the Internet more than ever before. Entire websites are now dedicated to the verifications of stories that are circulated through e-mails or appear on other websites. "Urban legends" have become so popular that books and movies have been created about them. Could it be that such things have happened around the life of Michel de Nostradame as well?

To find out, we must go to those who have specialized in his biography and writings. For example, let's take the interesting story of the three inebriated soldiers who lifted Nostradamus' coffin out of the grave which we read at the beginning of chapter one.

Did Nostradamus Predict the Date his Grave's Desecration?

> They raised the lid to see a sight that paralyzed them–across the skeletal remains lay a plaque which read 'May 1791.' Nostradamus, who had been buried two hundred years earlier, had incredibly predicted the *very date* of his exhumation.

Did this really happen? Here is what one source said happened at his death:

> Having left us with this final vision of harmony, Nostradamus died in

Salon in 1566 and was buried in the vault at the Church of St. Lawrence. His epitaph, translated from the original Latin reads:

> *Here rest the bones of the illustrious Michel Nostradamus, alone of all mortals judged worthy to record with his almost divine pen, under the influence of the stars, the future events of the entire world. He lived sixty-two years, six months, and seventeen days.* [27]

So the body of Nostradamus wasn't buried in a common grave, but was placed in a vault at the Church of St. Lawrence. If that did happen, then the executors of his will should have been incarcerated. The prophet's will states:

> Because after the soul the body is the most worthy thing at this time, the said testator has willed that when his soul has departed from his body, the latter will be carried to burial in the Church of the Covenant of St. Francis of the said Salon, and between its great door and the altar of St. Martha, where he has willed that his said body be accompanied by four candles, one livre each, and he has willed also that all his obsequies and funeral

rites be conducted at the discretion
of his executors hereinafter named.[28]

We find out more information from Edgar
Leoni in the biography section of the same
book:

> His body was to be laid in the
> church of the Franciscan monastery
> between the great door and the altar
> of St. Martha. For this, the friars got
> one crown. The executors were to be
> Pallamedes Marc, Lord of
> Chateauneuf, and Jacques Suffren,
> bourgeois.[29]

So it looks like those who put the body
into the tomb at St. Francis were well paid for
doing their job. Therefore, it seems that he
wasn't exhumed.

Here are more details from the same
publication:

> The soldiers of Revolutionary
> France seemed to have an insatiable
> craving for the violation of churches
> and tombs, and Nostradamus's
> tomb was no exception. In 1791,
> some Guardes Nationals from
> Marseilles broke into his tomb,
> quite heedless of the solemn warn-
> ing. One of them is said to have
> drunk some wine out of the
> prophet's skull. The bones were
> scattered during this drunken orgy

and the Salonians were only too glad of this opportunity to gather new relics. The Mayor, M. David, gathered together all the bones he could find, gaining the co-operation of the soldiery by ingeniously informing them that Nostradamus had predicted the Revolution. The remaining bones were placed in a wall of the Chapel of the Virgin in the Church of Saint-Laurent, Salon's other church, which escaped damage. In the interests of poetic justice, we are told that the "sacrilegious" soldier was killed the next morning in an ambush near Lancon.[30]

So the soldier didn't die at the scene. Instead, he was killed the next morning in an ambush. The author then adds another version that states he was caught with some stolen silverware and hanged. So it seems that there was no raising of the casket lid to see the plaque which read the exact date of the exhumation. It also seems that there was no dropping dead the instant wine from the skull touched the drunken soldier's lips.

Then again, we have a slightly different version from another expert:

> He died during the night of July 1 (1566), and was buried upright in the wall of the Church of the

Cordeliers in Salon. In 1791 super-
stitious French soldiers opened his
grave. His bones were reburied in
the Church of St. Laurent, also in
Salon.[31]

Yet another burial site? According to
Justine Glass' *They Foresaw the Future* the date
is incorrect. It seems that on the night of July
1, 1566, after the bout with gout, Nostradamus
made his last prophecy. He said, "You will not
see me alive at sunrise." He was dead right.
Let's see what Glass says about what
happened after the prophet's death:

Nearly fifty years after his death the
authorities of Salon decided to
remove his coffin to a plaßce of
greater importance in the church. In
the hope that other predictions
might have been buried with him,
the casket was opened and there, on
his breastbone, was a small metal
plate, engraved with the date of the
exhumation. He had foreseen even
that.[32]

So if we look through Glass' interpretation
we see clearly what happened. There was no
threat of a curse, no drunken French soldiers,
no drinking of wine from the skull, no shot
from a stray bullet, and it wasn't a period of
225 years until the supposed exhumation, but
a mere fifty years.

However, that may not be the true story either. The well-known psychic Mary Devlin first establishes that the prophecies of Nostradamus are "well-documented" and have "proven accurate to a degree far beyond the realm of chance." Then she says:

> Perhaps the most eerie of his prophecies was the desecration of his own grave. When superstitious soldiers opened Nostradamus's coffin in May of 1789, around the corpse's neck was a medallion bearing the very date of this disinterment.[33]

So, it was in 1789 that the desecration took place. That's 223 years after his death. Also, the medallion wasn't on his breastplate, but had been placed around his neck.

This now leaves us with three "well-documented" choices. He was either, 1) in a vault at the Church of St. Lawrence, 2) with the next door neighbor—St.Martha in the Church of the covenant of St. Francis, or 3) not in a coffin at all, but was sitting upright in the wall of the church of Cordeliers.

Another expert sheds more confusion on the incident:

> Tales had begun to spread concerning manuscripts or treasures allegedly interred within his tomb. . . So strong was the belief in these

legends that in 1700 the grave was opened by a gang of daring tomb-robbers. The robbers found neither treasure nor documents containing hitherto unknown Nostradamus revelations, but the tomb contained, as well as the bones of the seer, a thin, gilded medallion. On it were the letters MDCC, the Latin equivalent of 1700, the year in which the thieves committed their act of sacrilege.[34]

There is one more detail to add:

On his deathbed he asked his wife to have his body placed upright in the wall of Salon's Church of the Cordeliers. A rumor spread through the following centuries that a secret document existed inside his coffin that would decode all his prophecies. In 1700, the city fathers decided to move his illustrious corpse to a more prominent wall of the church. They took a quick look inside, careful not to disturb the body since they were aware of the quatrain warning against desecrating his grave. No paper was found, only a practical joke which had taken one hundred and thirty-four years for the punch line: on his skeleton hung a medallion with the year 1700 inscribed.[35]

So the incident wasn't 50 years, not 200 years, not 215 years, not 223 years, not 125 years, but it happened 134 years after the prophet's death. It was actually grave-robbers (or city fathers) that opened the tomb, not drunken soldiers. No promise of inheriting powers, no fearful curse, no wine drunk from the skull, no dropping dead, and no specific mentioning of the month of the exhumation.

By now it should be clear that there is no way to tell what exactly happened, or if it happened at all, but we should get an idea of how the confused facts got turned into the story we read in chapter one. Whatever happened, the story is typical of how reputations are made. Perhaps this tale made the prophet out to be a little more than he was.

Well, at least he was a great physician. At least he was a prominent healer "who would have stood out in history had he not made one prediction." Not according to one expert:

> He would seem to have been much more successful in treating victims of *le charbon* than most of his medical contemporaries. This was probably not because of any great virtue in the remedies he used in therapy, the formulae of some of which have survived. One of them, for instance, was compounded of rose petals, cloves, lignum aloes, and the dried and powdered roots of iris and sweet flag.[36]

Francis X. King went on to say how such a potion couldn't have helped patients at all, but what probably did help was the fact that Nostradamus disapproved of many of the terrible "cures" of his day and therefore didn't use them, much to the benefit of his patients.

What then can we be sure of in this story? Well, we know that Nostradamus died in 1566 and was buried. It seems likely that his tomb or coffin or grave was desecrated some time after to either be relocated or robbed. But what happened after that probably has more to do with Nostradamus' reputation than any actual happenings.

And what of the other stories we have looked at? How much faith can you have in the stories of the midnight visit of the queen to Nostradamus where she learned the fate of her family, of the pig-keeping monk, the wolf and the two little pigs, or the tale of the lost dog? The answer is that you can have as much faith as you want. If a tabloid claims: *Wife's Varicose Veins Form Map Leading to Hidden Treasure* or *Prophet Predicts Prepared Pork-Poor Pig Pilfered by Powerful Predator,* there is nothing to stop you digging deep into your pocket at the checkout stand.

It is almost as impossible to prove that a certain story didn't happen as it is to verify that it did, especially when you go back a couple hundred years. With time the details blurred, and when they are as important as they are to these stories surrounding Nostradamus, doesn't that make a big difference to the impact of the story?

For example, was there really a plaque or pendant in his grave? And if so, did it read "May 1791" or "1700," especially if the grave was opened in 1616? It is difficult to believe that any of these stories actually took place as they are related today, even if the people telling them are trying to truthfully relate the facts. And what if they are just trying to come up with the most fantastic tales to profit themselves or their cause?

But even if some or all of the stories surrounding Nostradamus' life turn out to be stretches of the truth, we still have his writings. Documentations are the most reliable way of telling the facts.

5

Experts Disagree

One fact of history is that legends build up around famous people. Did George Washington really chop down a cherry tree and then say, "I cannot tell a lie ..."? Was there really a second shot fired in the assassination of John F. Kennedy? Without a careful look at the documentation, it is hard to be sure.

As we have applied these principles to the stories circulating around the life of Nostradamus, we also need to apply them to his prophecies. Did

Nostradamus mention America in prophecy? Did he have anything to say about the beginnings and outcomes of the Second and Third World Wars? Did he mention Hitler? Did he foresee the assassination of John F. Kennedy? Did he predict the September 11, 2001 attack on the World Trade Center? What other foreknowledge has been attributed to Nostradamus' *Centuries*?

Was America Actually Named in Prophecy?

The rule is left to two, they will
hold it for a very short time,
After three years and seven months
they will go to war.
Their vessels rebel against them
The victor born on American soil.
(C4 Q95)[37]

This is taken word for word from *Nostradamus and the Millenium*. Incredibly, America is *identified* in the fourth line of this prediction by the great prophet. This is clearly the American Revolution between America and England. Ships are referred to and there is even an allusion as to who would win the war.

However, there is a small problem with the quatrain. Here is the same word for word quatrain taken from *The Complete Prophecies of Nostradamus:*

> *The reign left to two they shall not*
> *keep it long,*
> *Three years and seven months*
> *being past,*
> *The vestals shall rebel against*
> *them,*
> *The youngest shall be the*
> *conqueror of the Armorick country.*
> *(C4 Q95)*[38]

The author describes the *Armorick country* as follows:

> This signifies a Kingdom that shall be left to two, who shall keep it but a short while. Their title will be challenged by two Nuns.[39]

Here is the same quatrain from Edgar Leoni's *Nostradamus and His Prophecies:*

> *The realm left to two they will hold it*
> *very briefly,*
> *Three years and seven months passed*
> *by they will make war:*
> *The two vestals will rebel in*
> *opposition,*
> *Victor the younger in the land of*
> *Brittany.*
> *(C4 Q95)*[40]

Mr. Leoni makes the following interpretation of *land of Brittany:*

. . . or "Armenia." Rather doubtful, unless the quatrain concerns Turkish or Persian princes.[41]

The Naming of Adolf Hitler

Adolf Hitler was born in Austria, and earned a scanty living during his youth as an artist in Vienna. He joined the German army at the outbreak of World War One and served as a corporal in the trenches. When Germany surrendered in 1918, this stirred him enough to become involved in the political arena. He took over a small extremist party called the National Socialist German Worker's party, or the "Nazis." He failed in an attempt to seize power in 1923, was arrested, and placed in prison for five years. This was where he wrote his political philosophy, *Mein Kampf* (My Struggle).

Hitler held extreme nationalistic and racist convictions, with a blazing hatred for the Jews. But after the German economy collapsed in 1929, many German people began to vote for him. In 1932, the Nazis became Germany's largest political party. The following year, Hitler was appointed as the chancellor of Germany, soon eliminated all opposition and established himself as the Fuhrer.

In 1939, after having rebuilt the German military, he invaded Poland and launched his country and the rest of the world into World War II. During the war, he began his "final solution"–the attempted extermination of the Jewish people. He managed to murder six million.

After two years of war, he was the conqueror of most of Europe, but this was short-lived. By 1945, allied forces had defeated his armies. On April 30, 1945, he apparently committed suicide in his bunker in Berlin and the last of the German forces surrendered on May 8 of the same year.

Experts have told us for years that Nostradamus actually named this German dictator in his prophecies. Let's have a close look at what they say (these quatrains are taken directly from, *The Complete Prophecies of Nostradamus* by Henry C. Roberts– "The only unabridged, definitive edition of the authentic words of Nostradamus since 1672"):

In the year that is to come soon, and not far from Venus,

> *The two greatest ones of Asia and Africa,*
> *Shall be said to come from the Rhine and Ister,*
> *Crying and tears shall be at Malta and on the Italian Shore.*
> *(C4 Q68)*

This is the foundation upon which the "Hitler" interpretation is built. Hitler's name is the last word on the third line of the quatrain: *Ister.*

But look at the same quatrain through the eyes of another translator. This time from *Nostradamus and His Prophecies* by Edgar Leoni:

> *In the place very near not far from Venus,*
> *The two greatest ones of Asia and of Africa,*
> *From the Rhine and Lower Danube they will be said to have come,*
> *Cries, tears at Malta and Ligurian side.*
> *(C4 Q68)*[42]

Hitler has now become "the Lower Danube." But there is more evidence in other quatrains that this is indeed Hitler to whom the prophet is referring:

> *The great one of Mayence to quench a great thirst,*
> *Shall be deprived of his high dignity,*
> *Those of Cologne shall mourn him so much*
> *That the Great Groppe shall be thrown into the Rhine.*
> *(C6 Q40)*

There is the Fuhrer once again. He is here cited as the Great Groppe. If you are not a believer yet, there is further confirmation. This time it is an actual prediction that mentions Hitler and Mussolini, as well as Mussolini's flight to Germany after losing his power, then the eventual ruin of both of the dictators:

> *The year following being discov-*
> *ered by a flood,*
> *Two chiefs elected, the first shall*
> *not hold,*
> *To fly from shade, to one shall be*
> *a refuge*
> *That house shall be plundered*
> *which shall maintain the first.*
> *(C9 Q4)*

Finally, we see the death of Hitler, found here among the more than one thousand prophecies of Nostradamus:

> *He who by iron shall destroy his*
> *father, born in Nonnaire,*
> *Shall in the end carry the blood of*
> *the gorgon,*
> *Shall in a strange country make*
> *all so silent,*
> *That he shall burn himself, and*
> *his double talk.*
> *(C8 Q79)*

It seems that the truth has been stretched just a little for some reason. Others have also noticed this inconsistency:

> Some of these interpretations seem to involve a willful ignorance of historical fact. For instance, verses referring to "Hister" have been translated by some commentators as referring to Hitler; however Hister was simply the Latin name that Nostradamus used for the river Danube. Indeed in one quatrain, the seer refers to the completion of a bridge across the Hister.[43]

So if it is the Fuhrer, it seems that a bridge was constructed across his back.

The Dropping of the Atomic Bomb

On August 6, 1945, the United States dropped the first atomic bomb on the Japanese city of Hiroshima. As the bomb detonated, a white cloud like an enormous mushroom rose 50,000 feet into the sky. There was a blinding burst of light throughout the city. All that remained of Hiroshima was ruins and ashes. More than 80,000 people were killed in the immediate blast.

Many believe that Nostradamus is pointing to this event in the following prophecy:

Near the harbors within two cities,
There will never happen two
scourges the like of which was
never before seen,
Famine, pestilence within, people
put out by the sword.
Then cry for help from the great
immortal God!
(C2 Q6)

Expert John Hogue explains:

> The words of this quatrain, num-
> bered six, possibly after August 6,
> 1945, the day Hiroshima was
> irradiated, capture the prophet's
> horror while witnessing the two
> Japanese ports sacrificed on the
> altar of the dawning Nuclear Age.[44]

> However, Jean-Charles Fontbrune,
> the author of "the best-selling and
> definitive Nostradamus: Countdown
> to Apocalypse" interprets the same
> prophecy (C2 Q6) a little differently:

> [This quatrain] clearly predicts the
> Berlin Wall, which divides the city in
> two. Two cities near the gate.[45]

The Prediction of the French President Charles Gaulle (1958-1970)

In his book, *Nostradamus and the
Millenium,* John Hogue directly quotes

C9 Q33, where in line two the prophet actually mentions de Gaulle by name:

> *For three times one surnamed de*
> *Gaulle will lead France.* [46]

Here now is the same C9 Q33 from, *The
Complete Prophecies of Nostradamus,* by Henry
C. Roberts:

> *Hercules, King of Rome, and*
> *Denmark,*
> *Of France three Guyon surnamed,*
> *Shall cause Italy to quake and one*
> *of Venice,*
> *He shall be above all a famous*
> *monarch.*
> *(C9 Q33)* [47]

President de Gaulle has now become
three Guyon. Here now is Mr. Robert's
(Gualle-less) interpretation of the prophecy:

> We believe that the "Hercules"
> referred to the powerful and famous
> Napoleon, before whom all Europe
> quaked.

President de Gaulle is actually Napoleon.

But Edgar Leoni in his publication,
Nostradamus and His Prophecies translates the
same quatrain:

> *Hercules King of Rome and of*
> *"Annemark,"*
> *With the surname of the chief of*

triple Gaul,
Italy and the one of St. Mark to
tremble,
First monarch renowned above all.
(C9 Q33)

His commentary on "Gaul" is:

i.e., the surname of the one-time
(58-49 B.C.) ruler of Gaul, Caesar or
Imperator, title borne by the (Holy)
Roman Emperor.[48]

Take your pick: Gaulle, Napoleon, or
Caesar.

The Landing of Man on the Moon

He shall come to the corner of
Luna,
Where he shall be taken and put
in a strange land,
The green fruits shall be in great
disorder,
A great shame, to one shall be
great praise.
(C9 Q65)

Here is what has been called by some, a
"remarkable forecast" of man landing on the
moon. However, Edgar Leoni comments on
Luna: "The possibilities here are numerous.
Possibly Lunigiana."[49]

The Assassination of President Kennedy and Senator Robert Kennedy

In 1960, at the age of forty-three, John F. Kennedy became President of the United States. He was the youngest man ever elected to the office of President. He was born in Brookline, Massachusetts, and served in the United States navy in World War II, narrowly escaping death when the boat he commanded was rammed and cut in two by a Japanese destroyer. He served as a democratic representative for Massachusetts and was later elected to the Senate.

While functioning as President, he showed great fortitude during the difficult Cuban Missile Crisis of 1962. In 1963, he signed a nuclear treaty with the Soviet Union, and in November of the same year, he was tragically assassinated in Dallas, Texas.

Some experts maintain that the following quatrain is a very clear prediction of President Kennedy and his brother's murder:

*The great man will be struck down
in the day by a thunderbolt,
The evil deed predicted by the
bearer of a petition:
According to the prediction another falls at night time.
Conflict in Reims, London, and
pestilence in Tuscany.*
(C1 Q26)

President John Fitzgerald Kennedy was shot and killed shortly after twelve noon in Dallas, Texas, on November 22, 1963. His brother was killed a few minutes after one in the morning in California. It is said that Jean Dixon, one of the foremost psychics of modern times predicted his assassination as early as August 1952, eleven years previous. She maintains that she was kneeling before a statue of the Virgin Mary when the vision came to her.

The experts who believe that this prophecy is in reference to the Kennedy brothers also believe that Nostradamus indicated that the third brother, Edward Kennedy, would become President of the United States.

That's one interpretation. Here's another exegesis of the same quatrain from another expert, who says it was:

> The taking over of Czechoslovakia by Hitler, the resignation of President Benes, the dissensions over the matter between France and England and the dire warning of the consequences of this betrayal, are all remarkably outlined in this prophecy.[50]

The Space Shuttle Tragedy

> *Nine will be set apart from the*
> *human flock*
> *Separated from judgment and*
> *counsel: their fate to be deter-*
> *mined on departure.*
> *The unripe fruit will be the source*
> *of great scandal*
> *Great blame, to the other great*
> *praise.*
> *(C1 Q81)*

Few can forget the horror of the tragedy of the space shuttle Challenger. Here is the interpretation by John Hogue, the author of *Nostradamus and the Millennium* (he makes quick reference to the fact that there were seven astronauts in the Challenger tragedy, not nine as stated by Nostradamus):

> Except for the mistake in numbers, Nostradamus comes amazingly close in describing the greatest space tragedy to date. On January 28th, 1986, seventy-one seconds after liftoff, seven astronauts of the spaceship Challenger were killed when volatile gases leaking from the left solid rocket-booster enveloped them in a tremendous explosion.

NASA, the US space agency endured its own Watergate during the following months of investigation which brought to the world's attention flaws in design and command decisions leading to the launching of Challenger.

The US space effort was scandalized for sending their astronauts on the unripe fruit of faulty rocket-boosters in an effort to cut the budget.

During the same period the Soviet Space program continued to run smoothly with the complete support of its government and people to the other great praise.[51]

Here now is the exact same prophecy from the pen of Henry C. Roberts:

> *Of the human flock, nine shall be*
> *set aside,*
> *Being divided in judgment and*
> *counsel,*
> *Their destiny shall be to be divid-*
> *ed,*
> *Kappa, Theta, Lambda, dead,*
> *banished, scattered.*
> *(C1 Q81)*

Here is his interpretation:

The Supreme Court of the United States, consisting of nine members is here indicated, as well as the

Ploituro of the U.S.S.R. More than once has death and dismissal involved both bodies.[52]

Move Over Napoleon

While many apply the following prophecy to Napoleon (the first of three anti-Christs, Hitler being the second), it is said that the helmet far better fits Heinrich Himmler. This human monster apparently died while talking to someone:

> *The dart from heaven will make*
> *its journey,*
> *Death while speaking, a great*
> *execution;*
> *The stone in the tree, a proud race*
> *abased,*
> *Talk of a human monster, purge*
> *and expiation.*
> *(C2 Q70)*

Lady Di

Some claim he even saw Princess Diana (who he said would make it to her 73rd birthday):

> *She who was cast out will return*
> *to reign,*
> *Her enemies found among*
> *conspirators.*

More than ever will her reign be
triumphant.
At three and seventy death is very
sure.
(C6 Q74)

Because Princess Diana was tragically killed when she was still in her youth, it is no doubt claimed that it wasn't Nostradamus that was at fault, but our inaccurate interpretation of his prophecy, thus keeping his credibility intact. This is the reason his plausibility is still undamaged in the minds of so many. His prophecies are so mystical, so ambiguous, that if the cap doesn't fit one head, there are plenty of other heads to try it on.

Did You Miss World War III?

Other ace interpreters warned us that in the future, Russia would unite with America and triumph over the East after twenty-seven years of nuclear war. This Third World War would be worse than all other wars put together and would begin sometime between 1981 and 1999. If you are wondering if you missed something, you didn't. This obviously never happened, but it may happen in the future. Skilled interpreter Henry Roberts is silent on the issue . . . so I guess there isn't much there to play with. However, with war being "declared" on terrorism in what can be oversimplified as an East vs. West conflict, it wouldn't be difficult to believe something like this might take place in the next few decades. The Battle of Armageddon foretold of in the Bible, which most experts believe will be the culmination of a war between the friends and enemies of Israel, does seems likely to include nuclear and/or biological weapons.[53] Could it be that the attack on the Twin Towers will be the event that divides the sides for this last great battle?

The same authorities (commenting on C3 Q84 and C2 Q41 on a TV documentary made back in 1979 called *Nostradamus: Life, Prophecies, and Mystique*) said:

> These two quatrains clearly describe the destruction of Rome, probably by a nuclear blast. And if we refer to the figures acquired earlier, it seems safe to assume that sometime before the year 1995, the Pope will have to leave Rome, because the great city is devastated by an atomic bomb.

Future Joys

So, what wonderful things has humanity to look forward to in the immediate future? Here is another part of the future according to Nostradamus:

The great famine which I feel
approaching
Will often recur and then become
universal:
So great will it be, and so long will
it last
That they will eat woodland roots
and drag children from
the breast.
(C1Q67)

Here is the exciting interpretation from Francis X. King:

> It may be that Nostradamus was prophesying a famine of such severity that cannibalism will be practiced throughout the entire world![54]

Goodbye California

If you still trust in all the prophecies of Nostradamus, sink your trusting teeth into the following yet to be realized predictions:

Towards the south there will be a
great drought.
An earthquake will be reported
From the bottom of Asia, Corinth,
and Ephesus
In an unstable and troubled state.
(C3 Q3)

*For several nights the earth will
shake,
In the spring two great efforts
together;
Corinth and Ephesus will swim in
two seas. (C2 Q52)
The trembling of the earth at
Mortara,
The tin islands of St.George are
half sunk.*
(C9 Q31)

Here is the interpretation from John
Hogue:

Next comes the long awaited super
quake in the San Andreas fault
which will rock the west coast of
America. Seawater will flood into
the Southern California deserts
from the Gulf of California as the
west coast breaks away from the
mainland.[55]

The interpretation continues:

By the mid-1990s a second wave of
super quakes is generally foreseen.
By then the western United States
will have vanished or broken up into
islands. East Africa will split into
three pieces. South America and
Tierra Fuego also split apart. New
York City and Florida will be
flooded as new continent-sized

islands rise off the Caribbean, the submerged coast of Southern California and the South Pacific. New Zealand, Australia and Virginia in the United States are seen by modern psychics as safe areas.[56]

New Zealand is situated right on the Pacific Rim (the name given to the rim of faults upon which sixty percent of the world's earthquakes occur. New Zealand sits at the bottom of the rim). One quake there in recent years killed more than thirty people.

Separating the Wheat from the Chaff

At this point you may be disappointed with the confusion the experts have thrown into the analysis of the prophecies of Nostradamus, but don't despair. That is not the purpose of this book. While there are several irregularities in the interpretation of Nostradamus' writings, there is still some gold in the bottom of the pan. Which prophecies *did* Nostradamus get right? If we throw Nostradamus out completely, then we are throwing the baby out with the bathwater. What we must do is find a way to look at his work and separate the true from the false and the vague. As I have said before, a closer look a the prophecies of Nostradamus will reveal that there was one source of his prophecies that was sound. Once we discover that by further analysis of his work, we will have a method for separating the wheat (the good) from the chaff (the bad).

Yet before we can do that we need to explore a bit more the nature of prophecy and the place of prophecy for us today. If there is a way through God or the spiritual world in general to foresee the future, then that will provide us with another key for unlocking the mysteries surrounding Nostradamus and his writings. And if there is such a way to determine the good from the bad, then it will help us in the interpretation of any other predictions we hear. But first we must answer the question, "Are there still prophets today?"

6

Modern Prophets?

Spiritualism is no longer the forbidden zone of human exploration it was in the sixteenth century. That which was taboo in the past has become part of the daily life of contemporary America. Almost every newspaper and magazine carries horoscope readings for their subscribers. Psychics mass deliver emails with promises of a word about the future. Television parades celebrities who give enthusiastic testimonies about how they have been blessed by psychics.

What was once hidden has now been revealed even within the U.S. government. The CIA spent an amazing $20 million on psychics from 1975-1995, in an effort to gain intelligence.[57] We have even seen through the media that the wives of presidents have consulted psychics for guidance while in office.

At the beginning of each year, predictably, the news media parades a long line of those who profess to know the future. With hit and miss predictions, the procession moves from palm-reading to crystal-ball-gazing gypsies, to respectably dressed and clean-cut astrologers all done in an effort to bring some sort of clue as to what the immediate hereafter holds for humanity.

In the thick fog of the future, now and then someone says something that actually comes to pass. How do we tell the difference between the true and the false? What good is a prophet that is accurate less than half the time? I mean, even the weatherperson does better than that!

Jeane Dixon (1917-1997)

Perhaps you had faith in Jeane Dixon, America's most famous psychic. She was the woman who supernaturally heard of the coming assassination of President Kennedy, and who many believe was mentioned by Nostradamus in prophecy.

As a child she wanted to be an actress or a nun. Instead she became a living prophetess. She has been called "Washington's phenomenal seeress." Daily she received avalanches of fan mail from her world-syndicated horoscope column. Despite her deep involvement in the occult, she aspired "to spread the Christian Gospel" into as many homes as possible. Every morning, she carried her deeply felt convictions to Mass after rising to recite the Twenty-Third Psalm aloud from her window.

She had her palm read when she was only eight years old and the medium told her that she herself would become a great mystic. It was at that meeting that she was given a crystal ball. Here are the details from her biography:

> The gypsy woman continued, "Your child, Madam, is designed for great things. In both her hands she has all the markings of a great mystic."

> Lost deep in thought, she turned around and disappeared into her wagon. When she returned she had a ball in her hand–a crystal ball.

> "Here, my little one," she said softly, placing the ball gently into my outstretched hands. "Take it–tell me what you see."[58]

After the child described a rocky coast, a turbulent sea and giant waves, the gypsy was overjoyed and said, "Keep the ball. It is yours. It can do more in your hands than in mine!"[59]

Ms. Dixon, like Nostradamus was never at a loss for words when it came to predictions. She also (as did Nostradamus) prophesied of the coming of the anti-Christ, earthquakes, the second coming of Christ, etc.

But didn't her occult practices—her horoscopes, her psychic powers, etc., conflict with her Roman Catholic faith? Not at all. She, like Nostradamus, saw no conflict.

When questions have been asked about Nostradamus' conversion, one expert explains why he thought the prophet was a sincere Catholic:

> There seems to be no good reason to doubt Nostradamus' Catholicism, although, like a number of other occultists throughout the centuries, he appears to have found his faith quite compatible with the practice of ritual magic and other forbidden arts.[60]

Indeed Jeane Dixon says of her well-known horoscope column:

> The science of astrology was taught me as a child by Father Henry, a consecrated, dedicated Jesuit priest at Loyola University in California, and it was through his teachings as well as his exemplary goodness that I came to believe it is possible also to help people through such astrological knowledge.[61]

As with Nostradamus and other psychics, Jeane Dixon was convinced beyond a shadow of a doubt that God was speaking through her. In the prologue to her biography, she said:

> Each of us has a talent that functions as a primary channel of communication between the Higher Power and our self. . . . I believe that like a spirit that worked through the Biblical prophets Isaiah and John the Baptist it works through some of us.[62]

Later in the book, she added:

> Revelations are signs of the will of God, and not the will of man. When God reveals a future event through a revelation, nothing man can do will change it. The Lord gives a revelation to anyone whom He chooses, when He chooses, and how He chooses. A revelation has nothing whatsoever to do with extra sensory perception. It is God revealing His will, and when He chooses to use me as a channel for His revelation, I listen, I see, and I feel.[63]

Ms. Dixon's connection to the Catholic church may well have been the source of some of her prophecies, but not in the way it would appear. Look now at one incident that is typical of Ms. Dixon's insights:

Quickly I turned and re-entering the drawing room, spoke to the little dove in soft, caressing tones.

"Come here, little one," I coaxed. "Come and let me hold you."

Just as though he understood my words, he circled around again and flew directly to me, touching down gently on my outstretched right hand.

With the dove in the palm of my hand I slowly turned and walked back onto the terrace, talking to him softly.

The dove's unusual response to me attracted everyone's attention. All conversation ceased; every eye was on us, aware that something was happening beyond what they were seeing.

The dove nestled in my hand and watched my face intently as if afraid of missing one single word. His tiny black eyes never wavered but kept looking at me with great serenity.

Was he telling me something? I was not sure, but I stopped talking nevertheless and tried to concentrate with him on whatever his coming was meant to convey.[64]

This dove was apparently an omen. It was symbolic of the Holy Spirit. Look now at what happens when she tunes in to the spirit:

My mind's eye can often look deep into the far beyond, and my mind's ear can sometimes tune in to the far sounds of heaven, but this time I not only saw and heard, but felt—God omnipresent, God controlling, and God directing every capsule of time and space. Gone from my consciousness was the reception, gone were the people. . . . I was alone with the Eternal One, and felt reverently awed, and was experiencing again that beautiful unearthly quiet in the vast unending space of the great beyond.

Hardly conscious of moving, I stepped onto the terrace, the dove in my hand. People moved a little, off to one side, and to me it seemed as if the Red Sea were parting again.

It was as if I were not me—a mortal—any more, but a spirit of consciousness—off somewhere in vast, unbounded space, looking down the years at things to come.

I could feel the earth shake and tremble underfoot. Then it seemed as though the world had stopped rotating on its axis. I saw that this century there will be many geographical and geological change and many earthquakes. . . rivers will cease to flow and others will alter their courses. Where water is now, there will be land, and where there is land today, wild, swirling water will rush in and destroy everything in its path. . . .

Waves of thunder and lightening rolled in succession until all creation seemed to be echoing the same sound that enveloped the earth when He created it. And then there was silence . . . and suddenly I felt no longer alone. All sound had retreated into the great void, and instead peace and tranquility covered the devastated earth.[65]

This is indeed a most remarkable occurrence and the Biblical parallels–the dove and the parting of the crowd like the Red Sea–add more than just ambience to the story, but hint at the true "divinity" of the origin of her prophecy, although, as I said before, not in the way it would appear. What do I mean? Well, take a look at these passages:

For nation shall rise against nation, and kingdom against kingdom: and there shall be earthquakes in divers places, and there shall be famines and troubles: these are the beginnings of sorrows.[66]

and,

And great earthquakes shall be in divers places, and famines, and pestilences; and fearful sights and great signs shall there be from heaven.[67]

and,

And I saw a new heaven and a new earth: for the first heaven and the first earth were passed away; and there was no more sea. . . . And God shall wipe away all tears from their eyes; and there shall be no more death, neither sorrow, nor crying, neither shall there be any more pain: for the former things are passed away.[68]

Sections from another part of Jeane Dixon's autobiography? No. Passages from the Bible, saying for the most part what Ms. Dixon says in this prophecy. And the amazing thing is that this was coming true even as she was saying it. The twentieth century has seen an incredible diversity of earthquakes. Volcanoes (which cause geological changes) and wars (which cause geographical changes) have increased astronomically even since Ms. Dixon spoke these words. In fact war has become so common place in our world today, it isn't even reported in the news anymore.

But then, where was God when Ms. Dixon foresaw these things that were recorded and published in *Predictions* (Fisher and Commins) back in 1980:

· A comet will strike the earth in the middle of the 1980s, causing potentially disastrous earthquakes and tidals.

· Many will "die like ants" in the 1980s as a result of germ warfare unleashed on the Western world by Red China in alliance with Asian and African nations.

· More than a dozen African nations will take sides in a great war on that continent in 1987, the African equivalent of World War II.

· Intelligent life will be discovered on a sister planet "exactly on the other side of the sun."

The United States will have its first woman president in the 1980s.

In 1965, she told the *Reader's Digest*:

A child who was born in the Middle East on the 5th of February 1962, will revolutionize the world, and in due time unite all conflicting faiths and denominations into one all-encompassing faith. This child, which has been the subject of some of Jeane Dixon's strongest and clearest visions, comes from a simple farmer's tribe. She says, "Humanity will know the enormous strength of this man about the year of 1980, and his power will grow enormously until 1999, at which time there will be peace on earth for all men of good will."[69]

Apparently, Ms. Dixon learned more from Father Henry than just astrology, she must have also learned something of end-time events as prophesied in the Bible, for the accuracy of her prophecies seem more tied to that than any astrological tables. But then would she ever have become as famous if she went around saying, "Well, I was in my room the other night and I read the most interesting thing in the book of Revelation ..."

Even her remarkable prediction of President Kennedy's assassination wanes a little in the light of the following:

The idea that whoever was to be elected president in 1960 was destined to die in office had been, as it were 'in the air' ever since President Roosevelt's death in the office in the spring of 1944. This was because, as those interested in numerology had noted at the time of Roosevelt's death, since 1840 every US president who had been elected to office in the year ending with zero had died in office.[70]

Unfortunately there is a fast buck and instant recognition for those who can guess an unborn child's sex ten times in a row. Each year, a million psychics give a million prophecies about a million things. When one hits the mark, it makes headlines and establishes clientele. Too often, modern psychics are nothing but glorified fortune cookies—while you are looking for your fortune, they are making theirs, and there are plenty of hungry customers who are willing to part with their dollars to swallow the psychics mindless morsels.

If the Bible was accurate about diverse earthquakes happening worldwide, it may also be accurate in its warning that in latter days there would be an increase in people who explored the psychic world. It says that they will listen to "seducing spirits and doctrines of devils."[71] The same verse even predicts that those who do so will also have had a connection to the Christian faith. This sounds much more like the "familiar spirits" we spoke about in chapter two than God inspiring people with visions of the future.

Here are some more predictions from those who have called themselves prophets in recent years:

Irene Hughes

Ms. Hughes has been called "America's self-proclaimed first lady of the Para

Sciences."[72] Sometime during or before 1980, she predicted:

· Some form of nuclear war will break out within ten years.

· A United States president will die in office in the 1980s (the Zero-Year Theory again?).

· An oncoming ice age will be "very evident" by 1983 and fully upon us by 1989.

· The next pope will be assassinated and cardinals will rule the church until the papacy is no more in 1989.

· New York will be destroyed.

Though this last one may sound eerily like a prediction of the Twin Towers attack, please remember that only an area of Manhattan was destroyed.

Edgar Cayce

Edgar was called "America's Most Mysterious Man." He was a psychic who would lie on his couch in his study, fold his arms across his chest, close his eyes, and go into a state of self-hypnosis. He became so famous in the 1930s and 40s that 1,500 requests for readings poured in daily. Despite the fame and fortune, he was a quiet man "who studied his Bible daily."[73]

Amazingly, Edgar Cayce predicted the "creation of the State of Israel." But again, so does the Bible. He also predictably predicted earthquakes and famines, etc. He foretold of the destruction of New York, and like Nostradamus, he regularly used Biblical phrases in his prophecies. In fact, the authors of *Predictions* were amazed by his projections, saying they were "sprinkled with words such as Ye, Yea, Thy, and Hath . . . they sound positively Biblical at times."

Edgar was a family man. He believed in Hinduism's reincarnation, drank alcohol, smoked like a train, and "enjoyed the company of attractive women." Despite these activities, as well as his occultic dabblings, he was "a devout Christian."[74] He died in 1945, but believed he would humbly rejoin us in 1998, possibly as "a liberator of the world."

He certainly did *lie* on his couch.

Simon Says

Here is what psychic Simon Alexander said would happen after the 1980's:

- There will already have been, in the late 1980s, a nuclear disaster in the States which wiped out an entire community.

- South Africa will cease to exist.

- Pornography will be a thing of the past.

- Exploited sex will not be at all popular.

- No "super civilization" will be discovered on other planets, but contact will be made with a backward, humanoid form of life[75].

A Cause for Reflection

Despite the sincerity with which these people spoke, they were either deluding themselves or fooling us for fun and profit. No wonder, after spending $20 million of the American taxpayer's money, the CIA decided in 1995 to drop psychics as a means of intelligence. It took them an incredible twenty years to figure out that eighty percent of what the psychics told them was totally false:

> One Pentagon consultant working at SRI International wrote a ten page report predicting a massive air attack on Washington during one of Reagan's State of the Union addresses. . . .

He [another psychic] became convinced there was a Martian colony hidden beneath the New Mexico desert.[76]

Such predictions seem ridiculous to us in the light of history, but who could have told them in 1980, when most of these predictions were recorded, they were wrong?

Is there a way to tell a true prophet from a false one? I believe there is, and the method for doing so is wrapped up in discovering Nostradamus' most accurate source of prophecy.

7

Another Explanation

There are three types of people in the world–those who can count, and those that can't. The world is full of experts who make deductions, but their conclusion don't add up. This is the case with the accounts of Nostradamus' exhumation, his "brilliance" in the medical field, and with the "Hitler" interpretations.

Take for example the much–celebrated claim that the British used the prophecies of Nostradamus for propaganda during the

Second World War. Did this really happen?
Once again, it is based on truth, but colored
just a little:

> Nostradamus' persistent influence
> rests partly with his ambiguity: For
> years, people of various persuasions
> have managed to read something
> meaningful into his cryptic verses.
> During World War II both Germany
> and Great Britain enlisted the seer for
> their own ends. "Nostradamus
> Predicts the Course of the War" is the
> English title of a pamphlet produced
> by British Intelligence in March of
> 1943; the document was meant to
> cause consternation in the enemy's
> homeland by predicting Hitler's
> doom. The Third Reich already had
> come up with Nostradamus adapta-
> tions of its own and planned to airlift
> into France copies of selected qua-
> trains that supposedly forecast
> German victory. It appears the
> leaflets were never used, however,
> perhaps because of France's quick
> surrender, and the small number of
> British pamphlets smuggled into
> Germany had no appreciable effect.[77]

During the 20 th century and earlier, many
experts believed that Nostradamus said that
the pope who was in office just before the year
2000 would be the last.

Another clairvoyant priest (Saint Malachie) said the same thing way back in the year 1140:

> In the final persecution of the Holy Roman Church there will reign Peter the Roman, who will feed his flock among many tribulations: after which the seven-hilled City will be destroyed and the dreadful Judge will judge the people.

The *seven-hilled* City referred to by Malachie is apparently Rome. Francis King explains:

> The expression "dreadful Judge" is usually taken as a reference to the Last Judgment, when the living and the resurrected dead are to be sentenced to either eternal damnation or given the reward of eternal bliss. But it could mean a judgment of a different sort-some world-shattering event, or series of events, which destroys the Church. In either case, if Nostradamus and Malachie are in concordance, then the next pope is going to be the last."[78]

The editors of *Man, Myth, and Magic* confirm this interpretation:

> Destruction of Rome . . . the last one will assume the name carefully avoided by all popes to date, and will be known as Peter of Rome.[79]

This would have perhaps been a safe claim to make ten or twenty years ago, but if another pope is elected soon, then watch the scramble to reinterpret these sayings, let alone explain how they got the name wrong. Or maybe the next Pope will be Peter of Rome and that is really the one meant. Again, prophecies in the far future seem almost as safe to throw out as are prophecies that have apparently already come to pass, but what of things that will happen in the next few years? For that we need a more certain source. Books about the Y2K bug sold like hot cakes on a cold day in Alaska as 1999 progressed, but as of January 1, 2000 that changed dramatically.

So what are we to make of all this? We have looked at a lot of predictions where the experts confused the issues or gave contradicting interpretations of his writings. However, here is one that he got right—or did he?

The Great Fire of London

The prophet not only gave the date of the fire (1666), but he named London, and gave other details that English history tells us confirmed his words to a cup of tea. How could this be? Here is a possible answer:

> Still other quatrains that have been considered farsighted may actually refer to contemporary events with

which Nostradamus should have been familiar. Skeptics cite the quatrain that purportedly depicts the Great Fire of London, down to the date, "twenty-three the sixes," or 1666. (To arrive at the year, believers multiply twenty by three, add a pair of sixes, and note that it was common in Nostradamus' time to omit the first digits of a date.) The verse's forecast of a fall of a lady from a high place has traditionally been interpreted as a reference to St. Paul's Church, which was so ravished by the flames, it was torn down. But skeptics suggest that Nostradamus more likely referred to Queen Mary of England, known as Bloody Mary, who was at the time executing numbers of heretics, often in groups of six. Although Mary did not die until 1558, after the verse was printed, it would not have been particularly insightful in that turbulent era to predict a ruler's downfall or death.[80]

Again, the conclusions are uncertain. Could it be that the best place to interpret Nostradamus' writings is from a place sometime after an event occurs that somewhat matches something he said? This thought is well summarized by Jean Gimon in a book published on the history of Salon in 1882:

The style of the *Centuries* is so mul-
tiform and nebulous that each may,
with a little effort and good will, find
in them what he seeks. Like airy
vapor's, they assume, as they unroll,
the figures of which the spectator's
imagination lends them, and this
fact assures this sibylline work of an
immense and eternal success with
those who are devotees of the mar-
velous.[81]

It is true, the forecastings of Nostradamus
are often so vague, they can be shaped by the
hands of the wildest imagination. There are no
bounds as to how far they may be stretched to
fit. Look at this interesting stretch of the mind
from Elizabeth Greene in the preface of
Nostradamus Countdown To Apocalypse:

To Nostradamus a king meant only
one thing: the physical king of a
physical country. We, however, are
somewhat more sophisticated now.
There are not many kings left these
days, and though they rule, they do
not govern as they once did. Now we
have presidents and prime   min-
isters, juntas and governing commit-
tees. More fancifully, perhaps, there
are also inner rulers: dominant
ideas, governing our morals and
values, little petty tyrants of our
minds and souls, benign spiritual

leaders that we call our good will or higher principles. What if an inner king, rather than an outer one, retrieved his lost throne at the end of the millennium? What if the great war that Nostradamus foresees were a psychological battlefield, rather than a physical one? Like an image from a dream, the Great King ruling by right of heaven is open to many levels of interpretation, and they all occur at once.[82]

The phrase "we, however, are somewhat more sophisticated now," is more than just an inference that Nostradamus was a simpleton. It is her most necessary platform to explain how to make a prophecy about kings fit, when there is a shortage of kings upon which to fit them. If the handsome prince has to snap off a few toes to make the glass slipper fit, so be it.

Study closely the following captivating quatrain:

A founder of sects, much trouble for the accuser:
A beast in the theatre prepares the scene and plot.
The author ennobled by acts of older times;

The world is confused by schis-
matic sects.
(C1 Q45)

Here's the amazing interpretation:

In the latter times anti-Christian
religious fanatics will send the world
reeling into confusion with terrorist
attacks. A noble author will publish
a powerful book about these terrorist attacks, which will take place on
American soil. Those who accuse
the founder of the sect of these acts
of terror will be drawn into a long
and troubling war.

Did Nostradamus actually predict my writing of this book? Alas, though it might help my
sales to claim that he did, he did not. This
interpretation came from my own fertile imagination "with a little effort and good will." But
from this it is not hard to see that it would be
quite possible (and probable, knowing human
nature) that some might take Nostradamus's
works and, for the sake of some easy money,
interpret them as they like for the sake of sell-
ing some books, newspapers, or videos.
Though reputable organizations have dealt
with Nostradamus and his prophecies, you will
find that most of them focus on the aura that
has emerged around him rather than any solid
conclusions.

So are we to just throw Nostradamus out with the bathwater? Well, as the saying goes, just because there is counterfeit money out there, it doesn't mean I am going to throw away the money in my wallet. What about the prophecies that have come to pass? What are we to make of those?

8

Nostradamus' Surest Source of Prophecy

Look at these predictions of Nostradamus taken from *Nostradamus 2: Into the Twenty-First Century* by Jean-Charles Fontbrune:

The people will rise up to resist and attack those who would promulgate new laws; also it seems that the countries weakened by the Orientals (USSR, Poland, Romania, Czechoslovakia, Hungary, East Germany and Bulgaria) may be victims of Satan freed by the creator of infernal prisons, in order to bring to birth great Gog and Magog who shall wreak so much abominable destruction upon the Churches that the reds (Communists) and the whites (Moslems) shall thereby lose their judgment, power and strength, but their (Soviet) fleet will be weakened by the Westerners, and this country (USSR) will know a great desolation; her greatest cities shall be depopulated and those who enter therein shall serve the vengeance of the wrath of God.[83]

Then Jean-Charles de Fontbrune says:

This section from the letter to Henri should be compared with Ezekiel 38:

Son of man, set thy face against Gog, the land of Magog, the chief prince of Meshech (Moscow) and Tubal (Tobolsk) and prophesy against him. . . . And I will turn thee back, and put hooks into thy jaws, and I will bring thee forth, and all thine army, horses and horsemen, all of them clothed with all sorts of armor (tank divisions). . . . Persia (Iran), Ethiopia, and Libya with them; all of them with shield and helmet (Russian armaments) . . . Gomer (Turkey), and all his bands; the house of Togarmah . . . and many people with thee . . . in the latter years (before 1999) thou shalt come into the land that is brought back from the sword, and is gathered out of many people (the State of Israel in 1948), against the mountains of Israel.[84]

Then, with wide eyes and mouth, the French author says: "There is a remarkable parallel between Nostradamus and these two chapters of Ezekiel."[85]

His "Divine" Source

As we saw in the prophecies of Jeane Dixon and the others, the divinations of Nostradamus contain words and phrases such as "milk and honey," "tribulation," "anti-Christ," "pestilence," "latter" days, "God loosed Satan," "seventy times," "Gog and Magog," "trodden down," "fire and sword," "the sea shall be red," "great tribulation as ever did happen," etc. These are *biblically*-based expressions, betraying why these out of his many prophecies seem to have come to pass.

A 1981 Warner Brothers documentary about the life of Nostradamus confirms this fact:

His ancestors were Jewish; his family had converted to Christianity. So when his grandfather adopted him, he studied the Cabbalah (an occult system originating in a mystical interpretation of the Scriptures among certain Jewish rabbis) as well as the Old and the New Testaments.[86]

Why are so many of his prophecies so accurate? Because he merely hung his own clothes on the body of Holy Scripture, and when the body came alive, he claimed to be the creator. *Nostradamus' surest source of prophecy was the Bible.*

If you take the time to study the prophecies of Nostradamus, you will find that he, like the Bible made *continual* references to wars, earthquakes, famines, pestilences, and plagues. Just as the Bible does, he speaks of the King of Kings, and the King of Terror who will come in the sky. He uses biblical phrases such as "the blood of the just" and of blood polluting the land. As does the Bible he makes use of the number seven continually, speaks of "dust and ashes," and "fire and blood." Also, as do the Scriptures, he mentions fire coming from the sky, and speaks of "those at ease" being "cast down." He uses the famous biblical saying, "a kingdom divided" and refers to "the blood of innocents." He even adds a couple of biblical "woes" for good measure.

All around us we see confirmation of what the prophet said would happen. There is the undeniable evidence of wars, earthquakes, famines, pestilence, and plagues. The truth is anyone who is ignorant of biblical prophecy *will* be very impressed with the prophecies of Nostradamus.

The prophet did not, however, make any mention about false prophets and their direct relationship to deceitful demonic spirits. The Bible does:

> Beloved, do not believe every spirit, but test the spirits, whether they are of God; because many false prophets have gone out into the world.[87]

I am sure that Russia will attack Israel. If I publicly state that fact without making it clear that the fountain of my belief is the Bible, then when Russia attacks Israel, I too may be heralded in the future as a great prophet by those who are ignorant of biblical content.

Nostradamus didn't have extra sensory perception, nor was he inspired by the flame of the Holy Spirit. He was educated and secretly read the Holy Scriptures, something forbidden by the Roman Catholic church of his day. The church was already plagued with what it saw as the curse of Protestants, who were Protestants because they read that Book. He either omitted the true source of some of his prophecies because he was afraid of punishment, or else he was becoming too famous as a sooth-sayer, perhaps both. Regardless of this, Nostradamus didn't seem to have any problem with lifting sayings from other writings and claiming them as his own.

Take for example what Jean-Charles
Fontbrune said as he expounded on how he
thought Nostradamus "enriched" his prophecies in a chapter called *On Method* in his book
Nostradamus: Countdown To Apocalypse:

> I could imagine Nostradamus in his
> study consulting many erudite liter-
> ary, historical, and geographical
> works to codify the vision which had
> been vouchsafed him. I became
> even more convinced of this when I
> was confronted with the huge mass
> of documentation and the cross-ref-
> erence which I myself needed, first
> to understand the meaning of qua-
> trains, then to collate them with the
> historical events they were describ-
> ing.[88]

The author admits that many believe that
Nostradamus, in his letter to his son Caesar,
discloses his practice of literary theft (plagia-
rism):

> Many have speculated about the fol-
> lowing passage from the letter to his
> son Caesar: "Fearing lest various
> books which have been hidden for
> centuries be discovered, and
> dreading what might happen to
> them, I presented them to Vulcan."
> This has been taken to mean that

Nostradamus had a secret library upon which he drew for his prophecies, taking all the credit without acknowledging his debt.[89]

Undoubtedly, within this secret library from which he drew his prophecies and took credit for them, was a well-used Bible, which contained the sure to be fulfilled words of true prophets.

If Nostradamus combined his biblical knowledge of future events with one thousand other occult prophecies, there are bound to be a number which fit the bill. Discharge one thousand arrows into the air, *and some are destined to hit a target*, especially if God has already preordained that they hit their mark.

Nostradamus made prime time news with his predictions. Add to this the exaggerated hearsay of the verbal tabloids of his day, and you have a reputation, recognition, and booming book sales. Try it. Read the Bible; call yourself a prophet, add some of your own imaginations about the future, and if you say enough, as time passes you may even become famous and have people lining up to drink wine from your empty skull.

Are These Things Coming to Pass?

We are now going to look at some more Bible signs of the end of the age. As we do so, think deeply about the fact that these were written 2,000-3,500 years ago, and look at their incredible specificity. There is nothing at all vague about them.

1. False Bible teachers would be money hungry. They would be smooth talkers, have many followers, and slur the Christian faith (2 Peter 2:1-3).

2. Homosexuality would be increasingly evident at the end of the age (2 Timothy 3:3).

3. Earthquakes would be in diverse places (Matthew 24:7).

4. Stress would be part of living (2 Timothy 3:1).

5. Many wars would erupt (Matthew 24:6).

6. People would forsake the Ten Commandments as a moral code, committing adultery, stealing, lying, and killing (Matthew 24:12).

7. There would be a cold religious system, in denying God's power (2 Timothy 3:5).

8. Men would substitute fantasy in place of Christian truth (2 Timothy 4:4). This is so evident at Christmas when the birth of the Savior is lost behind the myth of Santa Claus.

9. Deadly diseases would be prevalent (Matthew 24:7). The worldwide increase in AIDS deaths is almost inestimable. Over 160,000 Americans die of cancer each year.

10. The fact that God once flooded the earth (the Noahic flood) would be denied (2 Peter 3:5). There is a mass of fossil evidence to prove this fact, yet it is flatly ignored by the scientific world because of its uncanny implication.

11. The institution of marriage would be forsaken by many (1 Timothy 4:3).

12. There would be an increase in famines (Matthew 24:7).

13. Interest in vegetarianism would increase (1 Timothy 4:3-4).

14. There would be a cry for peace (1 Thessalonians 5:3).

15. The possession of Jerusalem would be at the center of international turmoil. (Zechariah 12:3)

16. Knowledge (in Hebrew, "science") would increase (Daniel 12:4).

17. There would be hypocrites within the Church (Matthew 13:25-30).

18. There would be an increase in religious cults (Matthew 24:11).

19. The future would seem fearful to many (Luke 21:26).

20. Humanity would become materialistic (2 Timothy 3:5).

21. There would be many involved in travel (Daniel 12:4).

22. The Christian Gospel would be preached as a warning to all nations (Matthew 24:14).

23. Jesus said Christians would be hated "for His name's sake" (Mathew 24:9).

24. There would be "signs in the sun" (Luke 21:25). This is possibly a reference to an increase in sun spots which, according to the dictionary, are "dark, irregular spots appearing periodically on the sun's surface."

25. Youth would become rebellious (2 Timothy 3:2).

26. Men would mock the warning signs of the end of the age saying, "These signs have always been around" (2 Peter 3:4). The Bible even reveals their motivation, they love lust (verse 3). They fail to understand that a day to the Lord is as a thousand years to us.

> God is not subject to the time that He
> created. He can flick through time as
> we flick through the pages of a history
> book. The reason He seems to be
> silent, is because He is patiently
> waiting, not willing that any perish, but
> that all come to repentance.

Thank God that He hasn't left us guessing
as to where on the time scale we are in these
days. He has given one sign that brings to
culmination all these signs. All of these
prophecies we have looked at are merely a
forerunner of one final prophecy preceding
the Second Coming of the Lord of Glory, the
Messiah–Jesus Christ. The skeptics who say
that these signs have always been with us are
right. To a degree, there have always been
earthquakes, rebellious youth, famines, etc.,
but the pivotal sign to look for would be the
Israeli occupation of Jerusalem.[90] The degree
heated up in 1967.

Way back in 1860, when the Suez Canal
opened, the United Kingdom gained better
sea borne access to its important possession of
India. Their borders were becoming increasingly threatened by the southward expansion
of imperial Russia. Britain, by intervention in
Egypt and by a treaty with the small
Sheikhdoms of the Arabian Peninsula, made a
number of alliances to guarantee the safety of
its sea routes. With the collapse of the

Ottoman Empire following the end of the First World War, the occupying European powers carved up the area under a mandate system established by the League of Nations.

In 1920, it authorized Great Britain to set up a postwar government in Iraq. Britain drew the new country's boundaries according to its strategic needs, mostly around old Ottoman provinces. The foreign presence rallied the Iraqis, and awakened a sense of national pride that would eventually drive the British from Iraq.

After the end of World War II, thousands of Jews began to pour into Palestine. Zionists had pushed for the creation of a Jewish homeland there for many years. However, Palestinian Arabs resented the new settlers, and there began a friction that eventually caused the United Nations to propose dividing the British mandate of Palestine into separate Arab and Jewish states. Arabs strongly opposed the plan, but in 1948 when Great Britain withdrew because of high costs in policing that state, among other things, Israel declared itself a state.

We are so familiar with Israel today that it is hard to imagine how unprecedented this was. What other nation, after being destroyed, ever reestablished itself? And then to have done it nearly two millennia later? That fact alone would make many think that the hand of God was in the situation.

It was front page news. *The New York Times* carried the headline:

Zionists Proclaim New State of Isreal: *The Jews Rejoice*

Then on Thursday, June 8th, 1967, the newspaper announced what those who knew their Bible's had been waiting for for years: the Israeli possession of Jerusalem:

Israelis rout the arabs approach suez, break blockade occupy old Jerusalem . . .

Israelis Weep and Pray Beside the Wailing Wall. Israeli troops wept and prayed today at the foot of the Wailing Wall–the last remnant of Solomon's Second Temple and the object of pilgrimage by Jews throughout the centuries.

In battle dress and still carrying their weapons, they gathered at the base of the sand-colored wall and sang Haltel, a series of prayers reserved for occasions of great joy. They were repeating a tradition that goes back 2,000 years that has been denied Israeli Jews since 1948, when the first of three wars with the Arabs ended in this area. This wall is all that remains of the Second temple, built in the 10th century before Christ and destroyed by the Romans in a.d. 70.

The Israelis, trembling with emotion, bowed vigorously from the waist as they chanted psalms in a lusty chorus. Most had sub-machine guns slung over their shoulders and several held bazookas as they prayed. Among the leaders to pray at the wall was Major General Moshe Dayan, the new Defense Minister. He told reporters, "We have returned to the holiest of our holy places, never to depart from it again."

Again, to many it was of little real significance, but to Bible scholars around the world it was of unspeakable importance. The Jewish people, after over 1,900 years without a homeland, occupied Israel. In 1967, *they set foot in Jerusalem fulfilling the words of Jesus Christ spoken almost 2,000 years earlier.*

God warned that if the Jews forsook His Law, He would scatter them throughout the earth, allowing them to be put to shame, then draw them back to Israel. The Bible makes special reference to Jews being drawn back to Israel from "the north country."[91] The nation of Israel is the night-light on the clock of Bible prophecy. It shows us how close we are to the "midnight hour." David Ben-Gurion, the first prime minister and minister of defense in Israel made this statement:

Ezekiel 37 has been fulfilled, and
the nation of Israel is hearing the
footsteps of the Messiah.

Prophet's Predictions

The signs of the times are so obvious, even
casual students of the Bible can see that the
Second Coming of Jesus Christ, which even
Nostradamus spoke of, is near. Look at these
words from a publication to which I previous-
ly referred:

Centuries before the great exile of
the Jewish people more than 1900
years ago, Moses, Ezekiel, Jeremiah,
Isaiah, and others foretold that the
Jews would be thrown out of their
homeland to be dogged by privation
and persecution. The expression
"wandering Jew" was apt:

*And the Lord shall scatter thee
among all people, from one end of
the earth even unto the other. . . .
And among those nations shalt thou
find no ease, neither shall the sole of
thy foot have rest.*
(Deuteronomy 28:64-65)
As surely as the prophets predicted
the Jew's dispersion, they forecast
their return. Ezekiel's words were
fulfilled on May 14, 1948, when the

State of Israel was established in Palestine:

> *For I will take you from among the heathen, and gather you out of all countries, and will bring you into your own land.*
> *(Ezekiel 36:24)*[92]

But what about the attack on New York and Washington, D.C.? Were they part of the end-time prophecies Nostradamus pulled from his surest source?

9

The World Trade Center and Prophecy

Look at his words that were reported by the news media the same week the attack took place:

In the year of the new century and nine months,
From the sky will come a great King of Terror . . .
The sky will burn at forty-five degrees.

Fire approaches the great new city
. . In the city of York there will be
a great collapse,
Two twin brothers torn apart by
chaos,
While the fortress falls the great
leader will succumb,
Third big war will begin when the
big city is burning.

An even more detailed prophecy flooded
the Internet:

It has been foreseen that exactly
three hundred and fifty years into
the future,
Silver phoenixes shall strike down
the twin brothers of oppression
That carried the king's nation,
which shall bring upon the apoca-
lypse.
In the City of God there will be a
great thunder, two brothers torn
apart by chaos.
While the fortress endures, the great
leader will succumb.
The third big war will begin when
the big city is burning.
On the 11th day of the 9 month
that . . . two metal birds would
crash into two tall statues,
In the new city . . . and the world
will end soon after.
-Nostradamus (September 11, 1651)

Did Nostradamus predict the bombing of the Twin Towers in New York? Not quite. His actual prophecies don't say, "In the year of the new century and nine months," but

In the year 1999 and seven months,
From the skies shall come an alarming powerful king
(C10 Q72)[93]

Neither is there a mention of "twin brothers" being "torn apart." The prophecy actually says,

Two royal brothers shall war so much one against the other.
(C3 Q97)[94]

As for collapsing in the city of New York and the sky burning, this is as close as he gets:

The heaven shall burn at five and forty degrees,
The fire shall come near the great new city
In an instant a great flame dispersed shall burst out
When they shall make a trial of the Normans.
(C6 Q97)[95]

Nostradamus never even mentions the words "metal birds," "statues," "fortress," or "big war." You should also have been suspicious because of the date put on the quote: 1651. Remember, Nostradamus died in 1566. Plus, New York City is at 41° latitude, not 45°, though the state of New York's northern border is near 45° and most have traditionally interpreted Nostradamus' *new city* to be Villeneuve-sur-Lot in France (*Villeneuve* means "new city"), which is about 45° latitude.

So we see that Nostradamus' words were twisted to fit the day.

The Day of Terror

You are a worker on the 106th floor of the World Trade Center. You love your job. It's prestigious to say that you work in the Trade Center. The whole world seems to envy you. Everything in your office is high tech. The view of New York is breath-taking. High building-high wages. You love life with a passion. Everyone in your office is of the same mind. You all want to make money. You discovered early in life that money is the key to open almost any door. It promises a secure future. Each person in the place of work is of the same mind; everyone that is, except one geek. You don't know why he is even part of the staff. It's rumored that the only reason he has his job is because he is the son of the building's architect. What a joke! He is so deluded that he thinks his daddy designed the World Trade Center. *You really don't like him.* He's a walking wet blanket. He never laughs at adult jokes or looks at lusty pictures. The guy is a dork. His idea of fun is to study books on architecture. He has as much in common with the rest of the staff as a pig has with a porcupine. No, you don't like him at all.

It's September 11, 2001 just after 8:40 a.m. What's-his-face is sitting in his office as usual. Surprise! He's studying building structure. The rest of the staff is standing around the coffee machine. Once again, the geek is the subject of an office joke. Suddenly, there is a very loud roar of a plane's engine. It is so close. *Too close!* You swing around to see a sight that horrifies you. A huge passenger jet is heading for your building! Within an instant there is a sickening explosion and a massive thud that knocks you off your terrified feet. The plane hits somewhere below the 102nd floor. In an instant there is unbelievable heat. Black smoke fills the room. Smoke so thick you cannot see an inch in front of you! Panic grips your heart. *You are going to die!* Images of your loved ones flash into your mind. People are screaming in terror. Double-glazed "unbreakable" windows have burst out on one side of the office allowing a breeze to clear the smoke for a second. You see a sight that utterly horrifies you. People are on fire. Others are leaping out of the windows to their deaths.

world will laugh at the narrow path you have taken to follow the Savior. But where else can you go? The Apostle Peter once said to Jesus, "Lord, to whom shall we go? You have the words of eternal life."[102] The prophet Isaiah said that by His knowledge God's servant would justify many. He is more than the Architect's Son.[103] He is the Creator in human form.

Am I saying that the Christian path is one of blind faith? No. Absolutely not. I have already given you the incredible evidence of Bible prophecy, proving that its source is Supernatural and therefore can be trusted. Faith in Jesus Christ is not blind faith. It is an implicit trust, borne out of reason, and it can be cultivated through the words of prophets greater than Nostradamus. These were not nebulous prophecies thrown out by mere men, hoping that somehow they will find fulfillment somewhere in the future. These ancient prophecies are one hundred percent accurate because they are not just the words of men, but the words of men that were moved by the Holy Spirit.[104] Their incredibly accurate fulfillment proves that their source was Almighty God. They substantiate that the Bible is the Word of the Living God, and therefore its promises of heaven and threats of hell are one hundred percent trustworthy.

Down through the ages, men have tried to destroy the Book that accused them of sin.

While the Bible is the world's most loved book, it is also the most hated. Yet, despite the malignity directed at it, despite the ages that have passed, it remains unscathed to this day as the world's all-time bestseller.

Try an experiment. Say something that someone will quote tomorrow. I don't mean say something that Shakespeare or some other great mind of the past penned, but something original, from your own heart, and see if anyone even remembers what you said tomorrow, let alone quotes you.

There is no record of Jesus Christ writing down His words, but there is a record of Him saying, "Heaven and earth shall pass away, but my words shall not pass away."[105] Today, after two thousand years His words are not only preserved, but hundreds of millions live by them as their very code of life. Napoleon wrote about Jesus,

> I know men and I tell you that Jesus Christ is no mere man. Between Him and every other person in the world there is no possible term of comparison. Alexander, Caesar, Charlemagne, and I have founded empires. But on what did we rest the creations of our genius? Upon force. Jesus Christ founded His Empire upon love; and at this hour millions of men would die for Him.[106]

warned that the New York attack would produce "terror, terror, terror," and that it would be made on "man-made mountains" (an obvious reference to skyscrapers). He also said that "nothing would keep the city from dying." There would be "hidden fires" and "hot wind," and that "the great city will soon be quite deserted." He warned that "all the Kingdom of Christianity and all the unbelievers shall quake," and that "sucking children shall be dashed against the walls." He then climaxed with "almost all the entire world shall be desolate."

There is good news though for those who make it through to the "golden age of universal peace of one thousand years." That time of peace will last until the world comes to an end in the year 3797.[107]

Orson Welles was truly appropriate to host the documentary. He was the one who on October 30, 1938 (the night of Halloween) broadcast a live radio hoax. He simulated a news broadcast saying that extraterrestrials had landed in New Jersey. The prank truly worked. Despite pre-broadcast announcements that the program was fiction, "at least one million listeners were terrified. Across the country, families took flight, thousands prayed, and some others readied themselves for battle."[108]

He also did a convincing job for Warner Brothers. There were a few inconsistencies that any Nostradamus fan could easily overlook.

The documentary said that the Muslims would *combine with Russia* and attack New York *before* 1999. Still, it was eerily close to what happened on September 11, 2001. However, if the Muslim world was going to attack America, New York *is* the closest target, and her impressive skyline sticks out like a tall and sore thumb. It wouldn't exactly be logistically sound to send missiles around the other side of the globe to attack Los Angeles, or send one past New York to carry on another 3,000 miles to strike San Francisco.

Remember also that it wasn't *Nostradamus* who got that one right, *but one of his interpreters.* It was the interpreter who thought that Nostradamus was referring to Muslims and New York. It wouldn't have been too difficult to imagine a Muslim attack on the U.S., in the light of America's support of the State of Israel.

Add to that some impressive visual effects, Orson's awesome voice, and you've struck gold. There is one other little inconsistency in the documentary. Nowhere in any of the one thousand prophecies or in his letter to his son Caesar or the Epistle to Henry II does Nostradamus (even once), mention the words "man-made mountains," "nothing would keep the city from dying," "hidden fires," or "hot wind." *Not once.* It looks like Orson was up to his old pranks once again. No doubt the simple will also once again believe him. Warner Brothers were wise to put a "disclaimer" at the end of the documentary.

people are hoping will save them on Judgment
Day, God's "goodness," will be the very thing
that will condemn them. If God is good, He
should punish murderers, liars, thieves, etc.,
and hell will be their dreadful fate.

What a terrible place hell must be. If you
saw in the newspaper that a man received a
five-dollar fine for a crime, you could
conclude that his crime was insignificant. But
if a man received *multiple* life sentences, you
could conclude that his crime was heinous. In
the same way, we can catch a glimpse of how
terrible sin must be in the sight of God by
looking to the punishment given for it: *eternal*
punishment. Sinful, rebellious, ungrateful
humanity never bothered to thank God for His
blessings of kindness, color, light, food,
warmth, joy, beauty, love, and laughter so He
will take it all back from them. Instead of
showing their gratitude by obedience to His
will, they used His name to curse and mocked
His Word. Take the time to read what Jesus
said hell was like in the book of Matthew. I am
afraid for you. Please, look honestly into the
mirror of the Law, then seek the "water" that
cleanses every sin.

Am I your enemy because I have told you
the truth? If you don't believe what I am saying
about it, it means you think God is corrupt
(that He hasn't the moral backbone to seek
justice), that Jesus was a liar, that the Apostles
were false witnesses, that God's promises in

His holy Word are nothing but prefabricated lies; there is no greater insult to God than to call Him a liar. By doing so, you are *adding* to your transgressions.

Imagine if you reject the Savior, die in your sins, and find that what I have told you is the Gospel truth? Then it will be too late; you will already be judged for your sins. If that happens, and your eyes meet my eyes on the Day of Judgment, I'm free from your blood. I have told you the truth, but if you choose to ignore it, your blood will be upon your own head . . . you will have no one to blame but yourself.

Can you see your predicament? You are guilty of sinning against God Himself, and because you have a conscience, you sinned "with knowledge." Isn't it true that every time you lied, stole, lusted, etc., you did it *with knowledge* that it was wrong? On the Day of Wrath you will be without excuse. Many times the Bible warns that God will see that justice is done. If there is no punishment for murder, then God is unjust. He would be like a corrupt judge who turns a "blind eye" to the dealings of the Mafia.

Does the fact that you have sinned against God scare you? It should. You have actually *angered* Him by your sin. The Bible says His wrath abides on you, that you are an "enemy of God in your mind through wicked works." But let fear work for your good in the same way that the fear of jumping out of a plane at a great height would make you put on a parachute. Let your will to live open your heart to the Gospel of salvation.

In late December of 1995, a dog named Chocolate fell into the icy waters of the Calgary River in Alberta, Canada, after a passing train spooked it. As the terrified dog struggled vainly to climb out of the freezing waters, rescuers, knowing that the dog could only live for a few minutes, got in a boat and rushed to rescue the distressed animal.

As they reached the now exhausted dog, a man reached out his loving arms. But as he did so, *he was viciously bitten on the face by the dog that he was trying to save.* Of course, we can excuse the animal by saying that it was panicked, and therefore not in its right mind. In its desperation to save itself, it didn't realize that there was another trying to save it.

Learn a lesson from a dog. God is not willing that you should perish. You are sinking into the icy waters of death. Don't try and save yourself. Don't panic. Stop the struggle, and let God pull you out. That is called grace.

To make clear what an incredible thing He has already done for you, let's look again to civil law. You are standing in front of a judge, guilty of serious crimes. All the evidence has been presented and there is no doubt about your guilt. The fine for your crime is $250,000 or imprisonment. However, you haven't two pennies to rub together. The judge is about to pass sentence . . . he lifts his gavel . . . *when someone you don't even know steps in and pays the fine for you.* The moment you accept that payment, you are free to go. Justice has been served, the law has been satisfied, and what's more, the stranger who paid for your fine showed how much he cares for you. His payment was evidence of his love.

That's what God did for us in the person of Jesus Christ. We are guilty, but He paid the fine 2,000 years ago. *It is that simple.* The Bible puts it this way: "He was bruised for our iniquities."[112] . . . "Christ has redeemed us from the curse of the Law being made a curse for us."[113] . . . "God commended His love toward us, in that while we were yet sinners, Christ died for us."[114]

It was no small thing for Jesus to die for us. The only thing that would satisfy the demands of Eternal Law was the *suffering* death of the sinless Son of God. *What love God must have for us!* He suffered an agonizing death, so that you wouldn't have to be punished for your sins. His sacrificial death and resurrection means that you need no longer be in debt to the Law, and God can now grant you everlasting life if you obey Him. Death no longer has a legal hold upon those who belong to Jesus Christ.

Today, Not Tomorrow

What then should you do? Simply repent and put your trust in Jesus Christ as your Savior and Lord. Think of a man who has committed adultery. His faithful wife is more than willing to take him back, so what is the attitude in which he should approach her? It should be one of tremendous humility, asking for forgiveness, and determining in his heart never to *even think* of committing adultery again. That's how you should approach God.

Earlier I mentioned that there was something that could be even more convincing than the words of the prophets. That "something" is the voice of your awakened conscience. The Bible calls the conscience the "work of the Law" written on your heart.[115] By that it means that it affirms the truth of each Commandment. We know instinctively that it's wrong to lie, steal, kill, commit adultery, to fail to put God first, etc. The word itself means "with knowledge."

The conscience is like a smoke detector. Many don't like its alarming voice, so they disarm it. That's like a man taking the batteries out of his smoke detector because he doesn't want its alarm to waken him. The alarm's purpose is to show him that he's in danger.

Stay with me now, as we look again at Nostradamus and what the future holds for you.

11

Exploring Today's Psychic Phenomenon

There's one more "sign of the times" we need to look at to see where we are on God's time clock. Bear in mind that this is not a sign of the end of the world, as doomsday prophets would have us think. It is a sign of the coming of Jesus Christ, and of the end of this "age"–humanity's renewed interest in the occult:

> Now the Spirit speaks expressly that, in the latter times, some shall depart from the faith, giving heed to seducing spirits, and doctrines of demons.[116]

In the United States alone there is enough business to keep 10,000 astrologers working full-time, and an additional 175,000 astrologers working part-time. Halloween has become as popular as Christmas. Horoscopes are in almost every newspaper, with many top-selling books, movies, and rock groups extolling Satanism and other occultism. Perhaps you are not feeling well. For just $75 an hour you can have a psychic send "healing thoughts" to you from the other side of the country. Or you could call "The Witches of Salem Network," because "if you like talking to psychics . . . you'll love talking to witches." Teenagers may watch their own teenage witch programs on television. Fantasy books such as Harry Potter have put the occult into the minds of millions of children.

Psychics reveal "hidden secrets about love, life, career, money, luck, marriage, health, the future, and personal problems." You can even call the Reverend Johnny Love for healing power prayer. He's a "gifted spiritualist psychic." Through astrology you can "find your destiny" . . . "expand your horizons" . . . "unleash the power."

You don't even have to leave your home to find your own personal Nostradamus. In the comfort of your home, you can make a connection. Your own confidential psychic can give you your own personal reading over your own personal telephone. What's more, it's almost free. All it will cost you is $3.99 per minute and your eternal salvation.

Mixed Sources/Mixed Motives

As we have seen, many modern psychics, like Nostradamus, propose that their revelations are from God. But look at what happened in the Bible when those who had a foot into the occult world came to faith in Jesus Christ:

> Then some of the itinerant Jewish exorcists took it upon themselves to call the name of the Lord Jesus over those who had evil spirits, saying, "We adjure you by Jesus whom Paul preaches." Also there were seven sons of Sceva, a Jewish chief priest, who did so. And the evil spirit answered and said, "Jesus I know, and Paul I know; but who are you?" then the man in whom the evil spirit was leaped on them, and prevailed against them, so that they fled out of that house naked and wounded.

This became known both to the Jews and Greeks dwelling in Ephesus; and fear fell on them all, and the name of the Lord Jesus was magnified. And many who had believed came confessing and telling their deeds. *Also, many of those who had practiced magic brought their books together and burned them in the sight of all.* And they counted up the value of them, and it totaled fifty thousand pieces of silver.[117]

As soon as they received the Holy Spirit, they renounced their occult activity. Then they burned anything which gave them contact with the spirit world. This portion of scripture doesn't mention the word "divination," but in the earlier chapters, the Apostle Paul shows its origin:

Now it happened, as we went to prayer, that a certain slave girl *possessed with a spirit of divination* met us, who brought her masters much profit by fortune-telling. This girl followed Paul and us, and cried out, saying, "These men are the servants of the Most High God, who proclaim to us the way of salvation." And this she did for many days. But Paul, greatly annoyed, turned and said to the spirit, "I command you in the name of Jesus Christ to come out of her." And he came out that very hour.[118]

The spirit that possessed the girl was attempting to promote the belief that *God* was the source of both her and Paul's message. There is nothing new under the sun.

In an effort to equate the Old Testament prophets with the occult realm, Theodore H. Robinson, speaking of the manner in which the Spirit came upon them says:

> He might be mingling with the crowd . . . Suddenly something would happen to him. His eyes would become fixed, strange convulsions would seize upon his limbs, the form of his speech would change. Men would recognize that the Spirit had fallen upon him. The fit would pass, and he would tell those who stood around the things which he had seen and heard.[119]

There is no evidence at all of any of God's prophets going into "strange convulsions" or convulsions seizing "his limbs," or going into a "fit" when the Holy Spirit came upon them. I have seen many people who have been possessed by demon spirits,[120] and this is obviously a description of a *demonic* manifestation.

The commands of scripture make very clear as to how we should regard the occult realm:

Give no regard to mediums and familiar spirits; do not seek after them, to be defiled by them: I am the Lord your God.[121]

Why Believe a Liar, Even When He Tells the Truth?

Shakespeare reminded us that the Devil can quote scripture. He quoted the Bible to Jesus Christ when he tempted Him to become a satan-worshipper.[122] For thousands of years, the entity that scripture calls the "spirit that works in the children of disobedience,"[123] has seen Biblical prophecies come to pass. If a liar tells you the truth, it is because he is using it to deceive you—so that when he lies to you later, you will believe it. Satan knows the "signs of the times" better than the most avid of Bible scholars. In the case of Nostradamus or even Jeane Dixon and the others we have looked at, the "father of lies" deceived the simple by speaking some scriptural truths through a familiar spirit. It wasn't the first time he did it, and it won't be the last. However, in this case millions who are not familiar with those Biblical truths, have been hoodwinked by a pied piper playing someone else's tune.

Also like Nostradamus, Jeane Dixon and others like her have much to say about the Bible, about the church, God, prayer, etc., but comparatively little about the person of Jesus

Christ. Yet the test as to whether or not someone is speaking for God is their conviction as to who Jesus Christ is. A demon spirit will deny the incarnation of the Savior. It will refuse to acknowledge Jesus for who He is. Let's look at the First Epistle of John and the verses that follow:

> Beloved, do not believe every spirit, but test the spirits, whether they are of God; because many false prophets have gone into the world.[124]

How do we "test" a spirit to see if it is of God? Is it a false prophet, a demonic spirit, or is it the Spirit of God speaking through a genuine prophet? The following verse tells us how:

> *By this you know the Spirit of God:* Every spirit that confesses that Jesus Christ has come in the flesh is of God. And every spirit that does not confess that Jesus Christ has come in the flesh is not of God. And this is the spirit of anti-Christ, which you have heard was coming, and is now already in the world.[125]

In fact, knowledge of who Jesus is, is the very rock upon which the Church is built. When Jesus asked Peter who he thought He was, Peter answered, "Thou art the Christ, the Son of the Living God." Jesus answered, "Blessed art thou Peter, for flesh and blood hath not revealed this unto you, but My Father Who is in Heaven. Thou art Peter, and upon this rock will I build My Church."[126] The foundation of the Church is Jesus Christ.[127]

He That Blinds

If you are too scholarly to believe in the devil, then you are calling the God of the Bible a liar. It is *His* Word that uncovers the spiritual source of all evil as being Satan. We are told that he came to "kill, steal and destroy," that he blinds the minds and deceives nations. The fact of your irrational denial of a source of evil, when evil is so incredibly conspicuous in this world, confirms what the Scriptures say of his labors. The Bible is a resume of his corrupt persona. Here is a quick synopsis of his background, work, and character:

> He is called the father of lies (John 8:44).
>
> He is the prince of this world (John 12:31).
>
> He is also the god of this world (2 Cor. 4:4).
>
> He tempts to disobedience (Genesis 3:4).
>
> He is a slanderer (Job 1:9).
>
> He inflicts disease (Job 2:7, Luke 13:16).

He hides the truth of the Gospel (Matthew 13:19).

He inspires hypocrisy (Matthew 13:38).

He ruins the body and soul (Luke 9:42).

He induces lies and murder (John 8:44).

He is our spiritual father: we inherited our sinful nature from him (John 8:44).

He inspired Judas to betrayal (John 13:2).

He is like a roaring, devouring lion (1 Peter 5:8).

He is the prince of demons (Matthew 9:34).

He deceives the nations through sorcery (Revelation 18:23).

He has the power to blind the mind and keep it in darkness (Acts 26:18, 2 Corinthians 4:4).

He governs over the "principalities, powers, rulers of the darkness of this world" (Ephesians 6:12).

He has all power, with "lying signs and wonders" (2 Thessalonians 2:9).

The Bible has much to say about the devil. The Greek word for "devil" is *diabolos,* which means "false accuser, slanderer." The word is used thirty-eight times in scripture. In another eighty-one places the word *devil* and *devils* are found.[128] These are references to evil spirits or demons. There is only one prince of demons, but there are many demons. Demons are spirits, which don't seem to be able to materialize unless they operate through the possession of humans or animals.[129]

Here are some of the characteristics and work of demons:

> They are intrinsically evil
> (Judges 9:23).
>
> They are shrewd (Acts 16:16).
>
> They are powerful (Mark 5:1-18).
>
> They possess human beings
> (Mark 1:32).
>
> They have miraculous powers
> (Revelation 16:14).
>
> They can be exorcised from humans
> (Matthew 10:7-8).

When someone ignores his conscience and calls upon demons for "guidance," the demons will gladly oblige. All that is necessary for demonic possession is a seeking heart and an empty mind.

Demonic Deceit

Author Edgar Leoni said of Nostradamus:

> The two principal foundation stones for his prophecies are magic and astrology. From the evidence we have, it would seem that when the spirit moved him, Nostradamus would go up to his secret study, lock himself in, get out his magic paraphernalia including a brass bowl, tripod, and laurel branch, and proceed to go through the demon-evoking formulas prescribed by Jamblichus.[130]

Nostradamus was deceived because he practiced that which his own heart warned him against. Why would he *fear* if he knew he was doing what was right? He emptied his soul, mind, and heart, and that method was believed to help Nostradamus "overcome a strong barrier of fear which came upon him before he surrendered his will in the occultic trance." He embraced that which the Bible says is an "abomination" to the Lord:[131]

> There shall not be found among you . . . a soothsayer, or one who interprets omens, or a sorcerer, or one who conjures spells, or a medium, or a spiritist, or one who calls up the dead. For all these things are an abomination to the Lord.

Nostradamus didn't always use his standard procedure. Now and then he did work with "omens." An omen is a "phenomenon or incident regarded as a prophetic sign." Edgar Leoni expounds this practice:

> Omens to the right and left served to make him more sure of his convictions. One such omen is mentioned by Caesar (Histoire de Provence, page 775):

> *The year 1554 . . . I don't know what sad and unhappy events begin and follow creatures hideously deformed and prodigious. Scarcely had January expired when one saw born at Senas a monstrous child, having two heads, which the eye could not look at without some sort of horror: he had been predicted some time previously by those who had knowledge of the course of future events. . . He was carried to my father and seen by several persons.*

> This, and the birth of a two-headed horse near Salon forty-five days later, caused Nostradamus to declare profoundly that a deep cleavage in France was ahead.[132]

This is one way he found out what was in the future. Did he really conclude that this two-headed child was a sign from God? Why didn't God speak to him through a spirit rather than give some poor child a second head just to show Nostradamus a sign of what was a head? Does God do such things? I don't think so. The Bible tells us how God speaks:

> God, who at various times and in different ways spoke in time past to the fathers by the prophets, has in these last days spoken to us by His Son, whom He has appointed heir of all things, through Whom He also made the worlds.[133]

Since the Day of Pentecost we have the Holy Spirit: the "Spirit of Truth,"[134] who "leads into all truth."[135] The Word of God is a "lamp unto my feet and a light to my path."[136] The Holy Spirit makes the Word of God come alive.[137] Look now of whom the Holy Spirit testifies:

> But when the Comforter is come, whom I will send unto you from the Father, even the Spirit of Truth, which proceedeth from the Father, *He shall testify of Me.*[138]

Look at what Jesus further said of the Holy Spirit and prophecy:

> However, when He, the Spirit of Truth, has come, He will guide you into all truth; for He will not speak on His own authority, but whatever He hears He will speak; and He will tell you of things to come. He will

> glorify Me, for He will take of Mine
> and declare it to you.[139]

If the Holy Spirit was, as Nostradamus claims, testifying through him, why didn't He attest even once to the deity of Jesus Christ? The Apostles did continually. They preached the person of Jesus Christ. In fact the New Testament mentions the name Jesus and the title *Christ* an incredible 1,528 times! The Apostle Paul in one of his epistles refers to Jesus Christ by name no less than ten times in eight short verses. The Savior is the life's blood of those who are possessed by the Holy Spirit. He is "the Alpha and Omega, the Beginning and the End, the First and the Last."[140] You cannot separate the testimony of Jesus Christ from the spirit of prophecy, for "the testimony of Jesus *is* the spirit of prophecy."[141] This is so clearly evident when you listen to the world pray. Take close note of scripted prayers on TV with actors seated around a Thanksgiving table or at Christmas (the celebration of the birth of Jesus Christ) and listen for someone to pray "In the Name of Jesus." It never happens.

When the Holy Spirit inspired John to write the Book of Revelation, the Apostle wrapped it in the person of Jesus Christ. It begins with, "The Revelation of Jesus Christ."[142] The second verse says, "Who bore witness . . . to the testimony of Jesus Christ."[143] The book concludes with, "Amen. Even so, come Lord Jesus! The grace of our Lord Jesus Christ be with you. Amen."[144]

Why would the Holy Spirit exalt Jesus? The answer is in the Book of Philippians:

> Christ Jesus, who, being in the form of God, did not consider it robbery to be equal with God, but made himself of no reputation, taking the form of a servant, and coming in the likeness of men. And being found in appearance as a man, He humbled Himself and became obedient to the point of death, even the death of the cross. Therefore God also has highly exalted Him and given Him a name which is above every name, that at the name of Jesus every knee should bow, of those in heaven, and of those on earth and of those under the earth, and that every tongue should confess that Jesus Christ is Lord, to the glory of God the Father.[145]

Nostradamus speaks many times about the pope, the church, Israel, faith, the Scriptures, and prayer. In his epistles, his letters, and his prophecies, he talks of the Holy Spirit, of God, and of Satan, but there is a conspicuous absence of any reference to the individual of Jesus Christ. There are a few exceptions where he uses His name to describe the Roman Catholic church, or as a fixed reference point in history.

He does however, twist the words of Jesus to justify not giving his occult utterances to those who oppose his practices: "give not that which is holy to the dogs," saying that God has "hidden these things from the wise and prudent and revealed them unto babes."[146]

Signs and Lying Wonders

Whether in ignorance or with intention, if we mix the occult with truths of the Bible, we *will* be greatly deceived. The following verses say why:

> The coming of the lawless one is according to the working of Satan, with all power, signs, and lying wonders, and with all unrighteous deception among those who perish, because they did not receive the love of the truth, that the might be saved. And for this reason God will send them strong delusion, that they should believe the lie, that they all may be condemned who did not believe the truth but had pleasure in unrighteousness.[147]

If we prefer the darkness of the occult, rather than the light of God's Word, God Himself may give us over to that which we want. Look at the categories of those who are thrust outside of the Kingdom of God (dogs are here used metaphorically "of those whose moral impurity will exclude them from the New Jerusalem,"[148]):

Blessed are those who do His commandments, that they may have the right to the tree of life, and may enter through the gates into the city. But outside are dogs and sorcerers and sexually immoral and murderers.[149]

If we have chosen to follow God, we must leave the occult behind. But why wouldn't we anyway? If we have a "friend" who is continually lying to us to get our money or steal from us in some other way, isn't that someone we want to leave behind? Then it is best we do the same with the occult.

12

Wheat Toast, Skim Milk, and World War III

Think of how many people entered the World Trade Center on the morning of September 11, 2001 making plans for the day. Perhaps they thought of the joy of seeing their loved ones that evening. Many no doubt chose carefully what they had for breakfast that day. Wheat toast, skim milk. They wanted to live a long healthy life. Maybe they were going out during the lunch hour to a buy a birthday gift for a relative, or a wife was planning to meet her husband for lunch. They had plans for the future. I would dare to say that not one of them would have believed that that day was going to be their last day here on earth.

It's human nature to think that we are somehow like God. We delude ourselves into thinking that death is what happens to other people. When tragedy strikes in the form of cancer, or a serious car accident, we say, "I never thought that it would happen to me!"

Every day 140,000 people throughout the world die. If we could speak with each one, the majority would say, "I never thought that it was going to happen to me!" Please, wake up from your self-delusion. Face the fact that one day, perhaps today, death is going to happen to you.

I face that fact daily. As you read these words, I may be dead. World War III may have started or an earthquake did finally drop California into the Pacific or I may have had a car accident. But, whether I live or die, I am ready for the future. For me death is no longer a black chasm into unknown terror. Although I hate the thought of being separated from those I love, the *mystery* of death has been banished. It has lost its sting for those who trust and obey Jesus Christ.

Death is but a dark door that opens to eternal pleasure for those who know the Lord. Do you know Him? I'm not asking if you know about Him, I'm asking if you know Him whom to know is life eternal?

Those who have faith in Jesus Christ look on the Bible differently than how they looked on it before they were saved. No longer is it merely a history book, or even a book of incredible prophecies that have come to pass. It is a *living* Book. It is a Book of "exceeding great and precious promises."[150] It is a Book that provides comfort. It is a road map, a guide, a light in the darkness, and it points to Him who is the fulfillment of all its wonderful promises, Jesus Christ, the only-begotten Son of God, who saved us from the wrath that is to come.

During the aftermath of the New York tragedy, it was reported by the news media that some spoke about the incident as being God's judgment on the nation. This was interpreted by others as meaning that His wrath fell upon those in the World Trade Center because their lives weren't pleasing to Him.

This same question came up in Luke 13:1-4 when certain people came to Jesus and questioned Him about a tower that had fallen on eighteen people and killed them. Was it God's judgment on them? Look what Jesus said to them:

> Or those eighteen, upon whom the tower in Siloam fell, and slew them, do you think that they were sinners above all men that dwelt in Jerusalem? I tell you, Nay: but, except you repent, you shall all likewise perish.

Instead of saying that the eighteen had "bad Karma"–that they had got what they deserved, He warned that there is a day coming in which God will judge the world, and that they should get ready for that day.

God only knows when His judgment falls on individuals, as in the case of a husband and wife, whom He killed because they lied.[151] The bottom line is that if God had already judged each one of us for our sins, a tower would have already fallen on us before today. To date, God has been rich in mercy and hasn't treated us according to our sins. That's why you need to take to heart His fearful warning: "I tell you, Nay: but, except you repent, you shall all likewise perish."

What Is Your Response?

If the many prophecies of Nostradamus are true and many are yet to be fulfilled, those who believe them are left in the dilemma of how to respond to them. Nostradamus leaves them in a boat on the Niagara River without a paddle. He gave no escape instructions to his believers.

Not so with the message of the Bible. Its words were given to bring us to a place where we triumph over death itself. If you are still not sure what you should now do to be saved, merely bow your head, confess your sins to

God and repent. By that I mean determine to turn from your violations of God's Law. Read Psalm 51 and make it your own psalm—your personal prayer. If you don't have access to a Bible, you could pray something like this:

> Dear God, I have broken your Commandments. I have sinned against You. Please forgive my sins. I now turn from sin in repentance, and put my faith in Jesus Christ as my Lord and Savior. In Jesus' name I pray. Amen.

Once you have made peace with God, read the Bible daily and obey what you read.[152] Do this every day, without fail, and you will never go wrong. God will never let you down. John 14:21 says:

> He that hath my commandments, and keeps them, he it is that loves me: and he that loves me shall be loved of my Father, and I will love him, and will manifest myself to him.

Panicking Prophet

Look at these hopeless words from a contemporary prophet (said to be the "new Nostradamus"). Just after the attack on New York, he said,

> May God Almighty comfort those who lost their lives today. Since 1995 I have been warning the U.S.

Government and the world that 2001 was the year you would see the start of the Great War. Nostradamus warned the King of Terrors would strike from the sky near 1999![153] In 1995 the US Government falsely arrested and prosecuted me for my writings. I specifically stated in case 96CV1499 in an edict, that the USA would not exist as a nation in 2001. As you can see today, that statement has begun to be fulfilled! Where is the President of the United States today? He hides from the people afraid of his life. Where are all the commercial planes of the mighty USA today? They are grounded from fear! What has happened to the great USA stock market? It is closed! What has happened to the Pentagon? It is evacuated! What has happened to Washington DC? It is evacuated! What about all the great sporting events of the USA, what has happened to them? They are all cancelled! You know what I warned of for 2001 way back in 1996! The USA from this day is no longer the great free nation it was for over 200 years. In one instant the way of life in the USA has been changed forever! Skyscrapers are now all targets! Federal buildings are now all targets!

Major cities are now all targets! And the future only gets worse for the USA! Soon George W. Bush will strike the Middle East! That action will bring about nuke terrorism upon not only Israel, but Rome and Washington, D.C. Suit case nukes are in the hands of Osama Bin Laden. When suit case nukes go off, the USA will be destroyed for all intents and purposes. Wall Street will crash! People will flee major cities! Gone will be the way of life in the USA forever! I warned you all of 2001! Now obey! Obey the Torah! Move away from the big cities."

A sinful world has reason to panic. However, look at the calming words of Jesus to those who love and obey Him, regarding the fearful "signs of the times":

And when these things begin to come to pass, then look up, and lift up your heads; for your redemption draws near.[154]

As long as you trust and obey God I can predict your future with more certainty than tomorrow's sunrise:

The path of the just is as the shining light, that shines more and more unto the perfect day.[155]

Eye has not seen, nor ear heard, nor have entered into the heart of man the things which God has prepared for those who love Him.[156]

And we know that all things work together for good to them that love God, to them who are called according to His purpose.[157]

Conclusion

Immediately after the attack on New York, America began talking about God and country again as if the Bible and prayer had never been taken out of the schools. We had a National Day of Prayer. The hymn *Amazing Grace* was on the lips and in the hearts of many. Psalm 23 was soberly delivered from pulpits and the Oval Office. Politicians prayed openly and sang "God Bless America" on the steps of Congress. Prayers were said in schools and broadcast on national television. The name of Jesus was even mentioned and the ACLU dared not open its mouth.

As so many have said, it *was* like a Hollywood movie. The world watched in horror as the huge twin towers of the World Trade Center crumbled. Thick clouds shrouded the city. The 11th of September 2001 will live in infamy in the minds of Americans as does the day Pearl Harbor was bombed. "Terrorism against our nation will not stand," President Bush declared before leaving for the capital. Then he called for a moment of silence.

The questions on the minds of many were, "Where is God when tragedy strikes?" "Where was He when thousands of lives were taken in such horrific circumstances?" The answer to this is in the Bible. God's promised blessings of health and protection from enemies are dependent upon something America has forgotten. We have forgotten about it because the word is rarely used in contemporary America. That word is *righteousness*.

Abraham Lincoln said, "We have been the recipients of the choicest bounties of Heaven. We have been preserved these many years in peace and prosperity. We have grown in numbers, wealth and power as no other nation has ever grown. But we have forgotten God." [158] Most Americans believe in God, but as the Bible says, we "honor Him with their lips, but our hearts are far from Him." [159] We have made a god to suit ourselves. As a nation we love violence. We feed on sex. In the name of liberty, we murder our children while they are still in the womb. We blaspheme God's holy name without a second thought . . . and we have lost His blessing. Look at our moral state:

- Adultery: USA Today reported that fifty to sixty percent of married couples admit to adultery.

- Fornication: According to the Oklahoma State Department of Health, approximately one in five people in the United States, 45 million individuals, are infected with the virus that causes genital herpes.

- Rape: A Harris poll sets the figure at 380,000 rapes or sexual assaults that took place back in 1993. The Justice Department says that eight percent of all American women will be victims of rape or attempted rape in their lifetime.

- Pornography: UPI News, November 19, 1997 said that porn video rentals soared to 665 million in 1996, accounting for 13.3 percent of video rentals in America.

- Abortion: Centers For Disease Control and Prevention reported 1,267,415 abortions in 1998. It's been estimated that there have been 40 million since Roe vs. Wade.

- Theft: It is estimated theft costs the country $500 billion each year.

- Greed: Focus on the Family revealed that Americans now visit casinos more often than they attend professional sporting events. Collectively, they lose in excess of $50 billion each year to lotteries, horse and dog tracks, casinos, and the various other gambling venues.

- Murder: According to FBI statistics, over 18,000 people were murdered in 1997. It averaged more than 20,000 per year, totaling 200,000 murders during the 1990s. Over 100,000 murderers were never brought to justice.

- Drunkenness: Florida Alcohol & Drug Abuse Association estimates that the social costs of alcohol addiction amount to $100 billion per year in lost productivity and related health costs.

- Hypocrisy: The Barna Research Group found that sixty-two percent of Americans profess to be Christians, while the book, *The Day America Told the Truth* said that ninety-one percent lie regularly.

We have called America a "great country" without reference to the God who made her great. We raised the twin towers as tokens of our wealth and power, and they were leveled to dust and ashes. Our great country was humbled. One leader said that "America has been brought to her knees, but she will get up again." Perhaps she shouldn't. We were suddenly made aware of our vulnerability.

After the plane struck the first tower, a public announcement assured those in the second tower, "This building is not in imminent danger. Stay where you are." God forbid that the Church should say the same thing to this nation.

Before the horrors of New York, few would have tolerated public talk about God. However, the incident caused Los Angeles secular television stations to announce prayer services in different churches. This happened across the nation. They could not but listen to the voice of Christians everywhere, the only ones holding out hope while others are lost in fear . . . and we must keep speaking. We were born for such a time as this. It is in darkness that light shines. This unforgettable tragedy was the beginning of an unprecedented opportunity for the Church. Thank God that there are some who want to do more than give blood to the Red Cross. They want to speak of the Blood of the Cross. It's not enough to hear Psalm 23, without the words of the Good Shepherd, who gave His life for the sheep. They want to speak of God's amazing grace expressed in the cross of Jesus Christ. They want to do more than light a candle in the dark. They want to *be* a light in the dark. They want to raise more than the flag–they want to raise their voices. Their moment of silence has ended. Be one of those people who refuse to let their neighbors die in darkness.

Please remember to pray for the millions who are deceived by the occult. To them it is but a harmless and fascinating lifestyle. They don't realize their true state before God . . . nor their future:

> Now the works of the flesh are evident . . . adultery, fornication . . . idolatry, sorcery . . . those who practice such things will not inherit the Kingdom of God.[160]

> And they did not repent of their murders or their sorceries or their sexual immorality or their thefts.[161]

> But . . . murderers, sexually immoral, sorcerers, idolaters and all liars shall have their part in the lake which burns with fire and brimstone which is the second death.[162]

What Should We Do?

Look at this email we received (in respect to what happened at the World Trade Center):

> I really don't think that God allowed this to happen because we are "unrighteous" people. Jesus was a

righteous man, and God allowed him the worst suffering of all. Suffering turns people toward Christ.

It should be noted that God didn't "allow" Jesus to suffer. God caused His suffering. God made Him who knew no sin to be sin for us.[163] It pleased the Lord to bruise Him.[164] He was smitten of *God*.[165] His wrath came upon Him because we had transgressed His holy Law. A. N. Martin said,

> The moment God's Law ceases to be the most powerful factor in influencing the moral sensitivity of any individual or nation, there will be indifference to Divine wrath, and when indifference comes in it always brings in its train indifference to salvation.

It is not suffering that is a "schoolmaster to bring us to Christ," it is God's Law.[166]

After the attack on New York, America openly wept . . . but not for her sins . . . only for her sufferings. Unless the Church rises up and we see this nation changed through the power of the Gospel, America will continue to sing *God Bless America* and *Amazing Grace*. She will soberly recite Psalm 23, bury her dead, then go back to her love affair with alcohol, violence, pornography, gambling, adultery, blasphemy, the occult, abortion, her love of money, gay rights, and her resolute campaign to ban His Law from this land.

I am afraid, not for myself, but for this country, and any other country that turns its back on God. Daniel Webster said,

> If we abide by the principles taught in the Bible, our country will go on prospering and to prosper; but if we and our posterity neglect its instructions and authority, no man can tell how sudden a catastrophe may overwhelm us and bury all our glory in profound obscurity.

What can you do? You could go to www.raycomfort.com and listen (free of charge) to our sixteen tape series and equip yourself for the task of reaching the lost. Charles Spurgeon said, "We must school and train ourselves to deal personally with the unconverted. We must not excuse ourselves, but force ourselves to the irksome task until it becomes easy."

Or you could also (through the same web site) buy this book at a very low bulk rate and give it to your neighbors and coworkers.

I recently received an email that said: "Pray for Afghanistan." Afghanistan is probably the most anti-Christian nation on the earth, so I blocked the item and pasted it into a Word document, but when it came out of my printer, I got the shock of my life. I had failed to block the "P" on "PRAY," and so the headline read: "RAY FOR AFGANISTAN."

Praying for a country is sure easier than actually *going there*. I believe God is saying to the Church of America that we shouldn't just pray for America. *We should go there.* We should go to the highways, the byways, and the hedges and compel them to come in. . . while we still can.

This generation of Christians was born for such a time as this.

Take courage. We have God's help in this difficult charge, and we have the strong consolation of His exceedingly great and precious promise: "If God be for us, nothing can be against us."[167] No God-hating nation can stop us. No demon. No devil. No evil nation. If God be for us, nothing can be against us:

> He has sounded forth the trumpet that shall never call retreat

> He is sifting out the hearts of men before His Judgment seat

> Oh, be swift, my soul, to answer Him! be jubilant, my feet!

> Our God is marching on.

> In the beauty of the lilies Christ was born across the sea,

> With a glory in His bosom that transfigures you and me:

> As He died to make men holy, let us die to make men free,

> While God is marching on.[168]

End Notes

[1]John Hogue, Nostradamus and the Millenium (Garden City, NY: Doubleday, 1987)

[2]Jean Aymes de Chavigny

[3]Jean Charles de Fontbrune, *Nostradamus 2: Into the Twent-First Century* (New York: Holt, Rinehart, and Winston, 1985)

[4]Letter to his son Caesar

[5]Henry C. Roberts, *The Complete Prophecies of Nostradamus* (New York: Henry Holt and Company, 1985)

[6]Jean-Charles de Fontbrune, *Nostradamus: Countdown to Apocalypse* (New York: Henry Holt and Company, 1985)

[7]Ibid.

[8]"Epistle to King Henry II"

[9]"Letter to his son Caesar"

[10]Carl Gustav Jung was one of the original students of Sigmund Freud who became a leading psychologist of the 20th century. His theory of the *Collective Unconscious*, that somehow humankind as a whole plugs into an unconscious that has always existed and thus shares certain ideals or archetypes, was central to the fame of his work.

[11]Elizabeth Green, "Preface" in de Fontbrune, *Nostradamus: Countdown to Apocalypse*

[12]Francis X. King, *Nostradamus,* (New York: St. Martin's Press, 1994), 138-9.

[13]*The American Heritage Dictionary of the English Language*, 9th ed., s.v. "occult."

[14]King, *Nostradamus,* 140.

[15]Isaiah 8:19; 29:4.

[16]*Unger's Bible Dictionary,* s.v. "familiar spirit."

[17]See Deuteronomy 18:11 and Leviticus 20:27.

[18]See 1 Samuel 28:7-14.

[19]"Epistle to Henry II"

[20]Ibid.

[21]Fisher and Commins, *Predictions* (New York: Van Nostrand Reinhold Company, 1980)

[22]Greene, "Preface" in de Fontbrune, *Nostrdamus: Countdown to Apocalyspe*

[23]de Fontbrune, *Nostradamus: Countdown to Apocalyspe,* 440.

[24]John Hogue, *Nostradamus and the Millennium,* 80.

[25]Richard Cavendish, ed., *Man, Myth, and Magic*, Vol. 23 (New York: Marshall Cavendish Corporation, 1970), 3131.

[26]*Microsoft Encarta Encyclopedia 2000.* Redmond, WA: Microsoft Corporation, 1999. s.v. "Houdini, Harry."

[27]Fisher and Commins, Predictions

[28]"Last Will and Testament of Michel Nostradamus" in Leoni, *Nostradamus and His Prophecies*, 773.

[29]Leoni, *Nostradamus and His Prophecies,* 37.

[30]Ibid., 40.

[31]Guiley, *Harpers Encyclopedia of Mystical and Paranormal Experiences,* (Castle Books), s.v.

[32]Justine Glass, *They Foresaw the Future* (New York: G.P. Putman's Sons, 1969).

[33]*Horoscope*, January 1996, 48-49.

[34]King, *Nostradamus,* 17.

[35]Hogue, *Nostradamus and the Millennium,* 52-3

[36]King, *Nostradamus*

[37]Hogue, *Nostradamus and the Millennium*, 149.

[38]Roberts, *The Complete Prophecies of Nostradamus,* 142.

[39]Ibid.

[40]Edgar Leoni, *Nostradamus and His Prophecies* (New York: Bell Publishing Company, 1982).

[41]Ibid., 249.

[42]Leoni, *Nostradamus and His Prophecies*

[43]*Visions and Prophecies* (Alexandria, VA: Time-Life Books, 1988), 20.

[44]Hogue, *Nostradamus and the Millennium*, 89.

[45]de Fontbrune, *Nostradamus: Countdown to Apocalyspe*

[46]Hogue, *Nostradamus and the Millennium,* 93.

[47]Roberts, *The Complete Prophecies of Nostradamus*, 289.

[48]Leoni, *Nostradamus and His Prophecies*, 391.

49Ibid.

50Roberts, *The Complete prophecies of Nostradamus*, 17.

51Hogue, *Nostradamus and the Millennium*

52Roberts, *The Complete Prophecies of Nostradamus*, 36.

53See Ray Comfort, *Scientific Facts in the Bible* (Gainesville, FL: Bridge-Logos Publishers, 2001).

54King, *Nostradamus*, 98.

55Hogue, *Nostradamus and the Millennium*, 162.

56Ibid.

57Douglas Walker, "The Vision Thing," *Time*, December 11, 1995, 48.

58Jean Dixon, *My Life and Prophecies* (New York: William Morrow and Company, 1969), 58.

59Ibid.

60King, *Nostradamus*, 25.

61Dixon, *My Life and Prophecies*, 25.

62Ibid., 9.

63Ibid., 58-9.

64Dixon, *My Life and Prophecies*, 51.

65Ibid., 52-3.

66Mark 13:8.

67Luke 21:11.

68Revelation 21:1-4.

69*Reader's Digest*

[70]King, *Nostradamus,* 73.

[71]1 Timothy 4:1.

[72]Fisher and Commins, *Predictions,* 102

[73]Ibid., 75.

[74]Ibid.

[75]Ibid, 104.

[76]Douglas Walker, "The Vision Thing," *Newsweek,* December 11, 1995, 50. [77]*Visions and Prophecies,* 20.

[78]King, *Nostradamus,* 83.

[79]Cavendish, *Man, Myth, and Magic*, Vol. 23, 3131.

[80]*Visions and Prophecies*, 20.

[81]Jean Gimon, *Chroniques de Salon*

[82]Elizabeth Greene, "Preface," in de Fontbrune, *Nostradamus: Countdown to Apocalypse*

[83]de Fontbrune, *Nostradamus 2: Into the Twenty-First Century*

[84]Ibid.

[85]Ibid.

[86]*The Man Who Saw Tomorrow,* dir. by Robert Guenette, Warner Brother, 1981, videocassette.

[87]1 John 4:1, italic added.

[88]de Fontbrune, *Nostradamus: Countdown to Apocalypse,* xxxv.

[89]Ibid., xxxiv. Italics added.

[90]See Luke 21:24.

[91]Jeremiah 23:7-8

[92]Fisher and Commins, *Predictions*, 21.

[93]Henry C. Roberts, Updated by Robert Lawrence, *The Complete Prophecies of Nostradamus* (New York: Crown Publishers, 1994).

[94]Ibid.

[95]Ibid.

[96]John 14:6.

[97]James 2:7

[98]Proverbs 14:12.

[99]Ephesians 2:8-9

[100]John 8:12.

[101]1 Corinthians 10:13

[102]John 6:68.

[103]Isaiah 53:11.

[104]See 2 Peter 1:21.

[105]Matthew 24:35.

[106]*Napolean Bonaparte* (quoted in *Evidence That Demands a Verdict* by Josh McDowell)

[107]Nostradamus didn't actually say that the world would end in 3797. He merely said that was the date to which his prophecies extended (Letter to his son Caesar). He did well to get the "thousand years of peace" correct. He proved once again that he could read. But he didn't read his Bible thoroughly enough if he believed that the world would end in 3797.

The Bible uses the phrase "world without end" (Ephwsians 3:21).

[108]*Our Times*, Turner Publishing, Inc. Atlanta, GA. Page 275

[109]See 1 John 3:15.

[110]See Matthew 5:27-8.

[111]See James 2:10.

[112]Isaiah 53:5

[113]Galatians 3:13

[114]Romans 5:8

[115]See Romans 2:15.

[116]1 Timothy 4:1.

[117]Acts 19:13-19, italics added.

[118]Acts 16:16-18, italics added.

[119]*Prophecy and the Old Testament in Ancient Isreal*

[120]Ray Comfort, *The Power of Darkness*

[121]Leviticus 19:13.

[122]Luke 4:7

[123]See Ephesians 2:2.

[124]See 1 John 4:1.

[125]1 John 4:2-3, italics added

[126]Matthew 16:18.

[127]See 1 Corinthians 3:11.

[128]James Strong, *Enhanced Strong's Lexicon* (Ontario: Woodside Bible Fellowship, 1996).

129See Revelation 16:13-16 and Matthew 8:30-32.

130Leoni, *Nostradamus and His Prophecies*, 108.

131Deuteronomy 18:10-12.

132Leoni, Nostradamus and His Prophecies, 25.

133Hebrews 1:1-2.

134See John 15:26.

135See John 16:13.

136See Pslam 119:105.

137See 2 Corinthians 3:6.

138John 15:26, italics added.

139John 16:13-14, italics added.

140Revelation 22:13.

141Revelation 19:10, italics added.

142Revelation 1:1.

143Revelation 1:2.

144Revelation 22:21.

145Philippians 2:5-11.

146"Preface by M. Nostradamus to His People," in Leoni, Nostradamus and His Prophecies, xx.

1472 Thessalonians 2:9-12, italics added.

148Vine's Expository Dictionary of New Testament Words, (Old Tappan, NJ: F. H. Revell, 1940), s.v. "dog."

149Revelation 22:13-4.

1502 Peter 1:4.

151See Acts 5:1-11.

[152]See "Save Yourself Some Pain" at www.ray-comfort.com for principles for Christian growth.

[153]As we have already discussed, Nostradamus said the year "1999," not "near 1999." Neither did he say that the King of Terrors shall "strike." He said that He "shall come." perhaps during his secret readings of the Scriptures Nostradamus came upon verses referring to the One who is known in the Bible as the King of Kings, who would come in flaming fire. The Second Coming of Jesus Christ is mentioned in 1 Thessalonians 1:8: "When the Lord Jesus shall be revealed from heaven with his mighty angels, in flaming fire taking vengeance on them that know not God, and that obey not the gospel of out Lord Jesus Christ."

[154]Luke 21:28.

[155]Proverbs 4:18.

[156]1 Corithians 2:9.

[157]Romans 8:28.

[158]Abraham Lincoln, 1863, in declaring a day of national fasting, prayer, and humiliation.

[159]See Matthew 15:8.

[160]Galatians 5:19-21.

[161]Revelation 9:21.

[162]Revelation 21:8.

[163]See 2 Corinthians 5:21.

[164]See Isaiah 53:10.

[165]See Isaiah 53:4.

[166]See Galatians 3:24.

[167]Romans 8:31.

[168]Julia Ward Howe, *The Battle Hymn of the Republic*

If you enjoyed this book and think that its message is important, you could help us immensely by asking your local bookstore to carry the publication. You could:

1. Call the store (or stores), ask for the "book buyer" and say, "Do you have *Nostradamus: Attack on America . . . & and Other Amazing Prophecies?*" Ask if he could carry the book giving the publisher's name (Bridge-Logos Publishers: 1(800) 631-5802).

2. Mail the coupon (on the next page) directly to the store.

3. You could drop the coupon into the store.

4. You could give the book personally to the buyer, telling him that you enjoyed the book and saying that you would be grateful if they would stock it.

A Special Note to the Book Buyer

After the September 11, 2001 terrorist attack on New York, the BBC, and the *New York Times* reported unprecedented demand for any books on the subject of Nostradamus. This is because his writings were reported to say, *"In the year of the new century and nine months.../ in the city of York there will be a great collapse/, two twin brothers torn apart by chaos."*

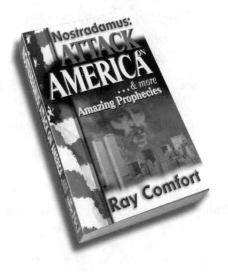

Thank you for taking the time to read this book. If you have found this publication helpful, feel free to call us for a complete list of other books, tracts, videos, and tapes by Ray Comfort:

For credit card orders call:

1(800) 437-1893 or (562) 920-8431

Or fax (562) 920-2103

or write to:

Living Waters Publications

P.O. Box 1172

Bellflower, CA 90706 USA

or visit our website at:

www.raycomfort.com

Also see the awarding-winning video from Living Water Publications:

Nostradamus: the Attack on New York . . . And Other Amazing Prophecies

Other publications by Ray Comfort from Bridge-Logos Publishers include:

How to Make an Atheist Backslide
The Evidence Bible
The Evidence For Kids
Scientific Facts in the Bible
God Wants You!